Take Control of Your AirPort Network

Take Control of Your AirPort Network

Glenn Fleishman

Take Control

Peachpit Press

TAKE CONTROL OF YOUR AIRPORT NETWORK

Glenn Fleishman

Peachpit Press, 1249 Eighth Street, Berkeley, CA 94710
510/524-2178, 800/283-9444, 510/524-2221 (fax)

Find us on the World Wide Web at: www.peachpit.com
To report errors, please send a note to errata@peachpit.com

Peachpit Press is a division of Pearson Education
Published in association with TidBITS Electronic Publishing

Editors: Tonya Engst, Adam C. Engst
Production Editor: Lisa Brazieal
Compositor: Jeff Tolbert
Indexer: Rebecca Plunkett
Proofreader: Ted Waitt
Cover design: Charlene Charles Will
Take Control logo: Jeff Carlson, Jeff Tolbert
Interior design: Jeff Tolbert

ISBN 0-321-32116-2

9 8 7 6 5 4 3 2 1

Printed and bound in the United States of America

Table of Contents

Table of Contents

Foreword

From Adam C. Engst, Take Control publisher

About a year ago, I gathered my nerve and began calling friends who write books about the Macintosh. "I have an idea…," I'd say, and then I'd describe how we could work together to address so many of the problems that plague today's publishing world. At the end of the call, as each friend enthusiastically signed on, I'd breathe a sigh of relief and dial the next number. I kept having flashbacks to those scenes in *The Blues Brothers* where Jake and Ellwood collect their musician friends with the deadpan line, "We're putting the band back together."

And thus Take Control was born. Take Control is a radical rethinking of how books are written, edited, published, sold, and yes, even how they're read.

Between me and my wife Tonya, Take Control's editor in chief, we've authored and edited more than 25 books over the last decade. We've written hundreds of magazine articles as freelancers and contributing editors for major Macintosh magazines. And we have 14 years of experience publishing on the Internet with *TidBITS,* a weekly electronic newsletter and Web site about Macintosh and Internet topics. In that time, we've received feedback from tens of thousands of readers, and while the vast majority of the comments have been highly positive, we've been frustrated by our inability to address common criticisms that were simply insurmountable within the limitations of book, magazine, and Internet publishing.

Every time we or any of our colleagues write a comprehensive book on a given topic, such as wireless networking, it quickly balloons into many hundreds of pages. But readers have told us that they don't like paying for or feeling as though they must read such large books. Also, even though those large books are good for reference, they quickly become obsolete, and people hate having to buy new versions. Magazine articles fall on the other side of the content spectrum from most books, and often leave readers wanting additional detailed information. And even more so than with books, magazines are here today, gone tomorrow—too often they're only ephemeral documentation that you can't easily refer back to later. Web publishing would seem to address some of these issues, but even the editorial sites that survived the dot-com bust have trouble generating enough income to pay the expert authors and professional editors necessary to produce the quality we expect from books and magazines.

TAKE CONTROL BENEFITS

The Take Control model helps you, the reader, in ways that were not previously possible by slashing through the Gordian Knot I just described. The key aspect of our approach is that every Take Control title starts life in electronic form, which lets us publish much more quickly than traditional books. Our first ebook, Take Control of Upgrading to Panther, was the first book of any type available for Mac OS X 10.3 Panther, since we released it at the exact moment—8:00 p.m. eastern time on Friday, October 24th, 2003—that Apple started selling Panther to Mac users in the United States.

Electronic books are still a new concept, which is probably why you're holding this physical book in your hands, but because you're entitled to a free electronic version of this book, our ebook approach will benefit you in numerous ways, including:

• **Tightly focused topics:** Let's face it, what you want (since it's what we want when we're buying books, too) is for a book to explain exactly what you need to know and nothing more. We address that desire by focusing every Take Control ebook on a specific topic. Since we're not attempting to cover everything, we can go into more depth than would be possible in a chapter in a normal book. Take Control ebook titles generally run between 50 and 100 pages, which we've found is a sweet spot for providing all the details you really need. It's difficult for traditional books that start and end their lives in print to be so focused because of the fixed costs of printing and distribution. (This ebook started its life around 80 pages and grew to about 150 after its first update.)

• **Free updates:** Print books start becoming obsolete the moment they go to press. Although many authors and publishers maintain errata lists on the Web, we've made an even greater commitment: we often update our titles to reflect changes in software and feedback from readers. Best of all, our updates are free!

• **No unnecessary typing:** Typing Web links and scripts from paper books is annoying, but it's easy to click them or copy them from an electronic book.

• **Better accessibility:** Not everyone can read small font sizes comfortably (or at all), but it's easy to enlarge the type in our PDF-based electronic versions, or even to use them with a screen-reading program. (By the way, if you need a format other than PDF, please contact us at tc-comments@tidbits.com).

- **The most accurate information:** Books vary in accuracy, as you've no doubt seen. We strive for the most accurate information possible, and to that end, we do some unusual things. First, our development and copy editors share in the profits, giving them an ongoing incentive to create the best possible book. Second, our titles benefit from a collaborative technical editing process that involves some of the world's best-known Macintosh experts checking each other's work. Third, if we find a mistake, we correct it in a free update.

Why then are you holding a print book, given everything we've said about electronic books? Because with our good friends at Peachpit Press, we believe we've come up with the best possible hybrid. The ebook in this volume has been user-tested: it has gone through multiple revisions and has helped thousands of Macintosh users set up and maintain AirPort networks.

Publishing this ebook on paper lets us give you a convenient reference guide in a familiar form that doesn't require you to read at your computer or print hundreds of pages on your own printer.

But as much as this book may be printed on dead trees, it's not a dead book, since your purchase entitles you to download the ebook version and any free updates we may release.

FREE UPDATES

I strongly encourage you to avail yourself of the free electronic version of this Take Control book. As I mentioned earlier, it's much easier to follow Web links from the electronic version than it is to type the links from these pages, and most important, we may update the electronic version to accommodate changes in the AirPort product line or wireless networking technology from Apple (we include a change list so you know what's new).

To download your electronic version, first visit this Web page: http://www.tidbits.com/takecontrol/peachpit/airport.html.

Once you're there, follow the instructions on that page to download the electronic version of this book. Note that you can sign up to be notified of free updates via email. If you prefer not to be notified by email, you can click the Check for Updates button on the cover of the ebook to see if we've released an update.

TIME TO TAKE CONTROL!

On behalf of everyone who has devoted time to making Take Control successful, I want to thank you for purchasing this book. We've all worked hard to bring you the highest-quality documentation about Panther that you'll find anywhere, and we sincerely appreciate your support. If you have any questions or comments, you can contact us via email at tc-comments@tidbits.com.

Finally, if you like what you read in this book, I encourage you to look for our other Take Control collections published in association with Peachpit Press, including:

- *Take Control of Panther, Volume 1,* by Joe Kissell, Matt Neuburg, Kirk McElhearn, and Glenn Fleishman
- *Take Control of Apple Mail,* by Joe Kissell

Also be sure to check out the many other Take Control titles we've published in electronic form. We've put a lot of effort into making the onscreen reading experience as good as possible (lots of links, readable font sizes, and no unnecessary scrolling), and if you prefer paper, our layout prints well too. You can find these titles (and more) for sale at http://www.tidbits.com/takecontrol/.

- *Take Control of Upgrading to Panther,* by Joe Kissell
- *Take Control of Customizing Panther,* by Matt Neuburg
- *Take Control of Users & Accounts in Panther,* by Kirk McElhearn
- *Take Control of Sharing Files in Panther,* by Glenn Fleishman
- *Take Control of Email with Apple Mail,* by Joe Kissell
- *Take Control of Spam with Apple Mail,* by Joe Kissell
- *Take Control of Making Music with GarageBand,* by Jeff Tolbert
- *Take Control of Buying a Mac,* by Adam C. Engst
- *Take Control of What's New in Entourage 2004,* by Tom Negrino
- *Take Control of What's New in Word 2004,* by Matt Neuburg
- *Take Control of What's New in Word 2004: Advanced Editing and Formatting,* by Matt Neuburg

Take Control of Your AirPort Network

by Glenn Fleishman

Contents

Introduction

Apple introduced wireless networking to the world with AirPort in 1999. Although corporations had been using forms of wireless networking for warehouse tracking and to connect buildings in a large campus, the cost was high, speeds were low, and complexity was manifest. Other companies were selling similar wireless hardware in 1999, but Apple's product shot off the shelves due to its extremely low initial price (especially in comparison to the competition), its simple configuration interface, and its excellent performance.

AirPort came out of the same approach that allowed Apple to ship the iMac the year before: taking parts that were available and standard, and combining them in a unique package that provided more value than any of the parts.

The AirPort Card fit into a special slot in Macs; its stand-alone, central coordinating hub was called the AirPort Base Station. The original AirPort line was superceded and supplemented in 2003 with AirPort Extreme, a faster and backward-compatible version. Most recently, Apple added its least expensive base station ever, the AirPort Express, which bundles several features into a unique package for home and traveling users.

Despite Apple's 5-year history with wireless networking and the general excellence of their software and support, I still find the same questions asked again and again. This book addresses these concerns and gives you tips that should save time, improve security, extend range, and give you a technical edge when working with AirPort networks.

Although the title of this book references AirPort, the book not only covers AirPort, AirPort Extreme, and AirPort Express equipment, but also includes many tips about comparable equipment or connecting to non-AirPort networks or from non-AirPort equipment.

I start with purchasing decisions, move through installation and configuration, give advice on the common task of extending the range of a home or small-office network, and finish with how-to information on security for those who want to make their AirPort networks free from interception. Several appendixes cover in-depth configuration of specific software and hardware, including AirPort Express.

AirPort Networking Quick Start

This book takes you through the process of deciding which equipment to purchase and configuring it to meet your needs, including how to set up larger networks and how to secure your networks against snooping and interception.

Wireless basics:

- Get a quick grounding in wireless terminology and technology. See *Wireless Basics*.

Pick a base station:

- Decide if one of Apple's AirPort base stations is right for you or if you want to check into other options. See *Consider an AirPort Extreme or AirPort Express* and *Decide What to Buy*.

- Disregard buying an older AirPort Base Station. See *Don't Buy Older AirPort Base Stations*.

- Learn the pros and cons of using a software-based base station. See *Consider a Software Base Station* and *Appendix B: Setting up a Software Base Station*.

- Pick a cheaper alternative wireless gateway if you don't need AirPort's unique features. See *Consider a Wireless Gateway Alternative* and *Buy Subsequent Access Points More Cheaply*.

Install your base station:

- *Pick the Right Place for Your Base Station* by testing signal strength.

- Install an AirPort Express. See *Appendix A: Setting up AirPort Express*.

- If you want to configure the base station to connect to your ISP, read *Setting up an Internet Connection*, where you will find lots of advice, including help with how to *Take Control of Dynamically Assigned Addresses*. Plus, *Pass Traffic to Individual Computers on a Private Network* explains how to allow traffic to reach servers and game systems on your local network.

- If you've attached a USB printer to your AirPort, configure your Mac or Windows XP computer to print to it in *Setting up a Shared USB Printer*.

- Learn about using the AirPort Management Utility to handle more sophisticated settings or configure multiple base stations at once. See *Appendix D: AirPort Management Tools*.

Improve coverage area and range:

- Add access points for roaming. See *Add Additional Access Points for Roaming.*

- *Bridge Wirelessly* among access points, in order to avoid wiring.

- Extend your network with a data network over your home electrical system. See *Extend with HomePlug.*

- Consider adding an antenna. See *Add an Antenna.*

- Learn how to *Solve the Titanium PowerBook Range Problem.*

- Solve interference problems by talking to your neighbors. See *Talk to Your Neighbors.*

Secure your network:

- Decide if you need encryption. See *Likelihood, Liability, and Lost Opportunity.*

- Apply encryption using an older or a newer method. See *Protect with WEP* and *Protect More Easily with WPA.*

- Choose to encrypt just data from applications instead of the whole wireless network. See *Deploy Application Security.*

Wireless Basics

Let's quickly run through some wireless basics to set the stage for what follows.

You might have heard of AirPort and AirPort Extreme by the name Wi-Fi, which is a certification guarantee for which The Wi-Fi Alliance trade group owns the rights and controls the testing. Wi-Fi loosely means wireless fidelity, in the sense of faithfulness: devices with Wi-Fi stamped on them work with other Wi-Fi devices, or are faithful to one another. I use the terms, "AirPort," "AirPort Extreme," and "Wi-Fi" interchangeably unless the distinction is important. AirPort and Wi-Fi networks need two parts: a wireless adapter that connects inside or outside a computer or a handheld device, and a wireless hub, like an Ethernet switch, that's known generically as an "access point" or "wireless gateway" depending on its features, but is called a "base station" in the Mac world.

The wireless adapter uses client software on the computer or handheld device to connect to a specific base station after a user selects the base station from a list or enters its name. Mac OS X allows base-station selection from the AirPort menu in the menu bar, the AirPort tab of the Internet Connect program (located in the Applications folder), and the AirPort tab assigned to the AirPort adapter in the Network preference pane. (If you're using a non-AirPort card, you may have to use a separate preference pane supplied by the card's maker or a third-party company providing a Mac OS X driver.)

When a wireless card connects to a base station, it's called *association*. If a base station has encryption enabled, then you must enter an encryption key exactly as it was entered on the base station in order to join the network after associating with the base station. Once a card associates with a base station, Mac OS X can carry out the next steps, such as automatically requesting an Internet protocol (IP) address using DHCP and sending data over the wireless network.

TIP   If you have no background in Wi-Fi and need more fundamentals, you can turn to *The Wireless Networking Starter Kit*, a 500-plus-page book written by Adam Engst and me that's available in electronic and print editions from http://wireless-starter-kit.com/.

EARLY AIRPORT

The original, slower form of AirPort and Wi-Fi is known as IEEE 802.11b. It sounds less technical when you learn that IEEE is the Institute of Electrical and Electronics Engineers; 802 is the number of their group that makes standards for local area networks (LANs); 11 covers wireless LANs; and, finally, "b" is the name of the task group that created the 11 megabit-per-second (Mbps) standard. Informally, 802.11b is sometimes called just "B," especially when you're using the term over and over—and over—again.

The original AirPort system comprises an AirPort Card, which fits into an internal card slot in all AirPort-capable Macs (the slot looks like— but is electrically different from—a PC Card slot); and an AirPort Base Station, which has three status lights on its front top and looks like a small, gray ("graphite" original) or white ("snow" revision) flying saucer.

The "graphite" base station has a single Ethernet port and a built-in modem. The "snow" base station added a second Ethernet port, which increased security and flexibility by allowing you to separate a LAN from a broadband or wide area network (WAN) connection via a cable or DSL modem.

AIRPORT EXTREME

In 2003, Apple added the AirPort Extreme system. AirPort Extreme uses the 802.11g standard, which the Wi-Fi Alliance added to the Wi-Fi specification. 802.11g is backward compatible: it incorporates all of 802.11b and adds speeds up to 54 Mbps. The 802.11g standard is often nicknamed "G."

AirPort Extreme uses an AirPort Extreme Card (it fits in a mini-PCI-like internal slot) and the AirPort Extreme Base Station (**Figure 1**), which now comes in two configurations, discussed ahead in *Pick a Base Station*.

The AirPort Extreme Card fits only into Macs made starting in January 2003. From January to September, Apple slowly phased the card into existing products. Simple rule: if it accepts an AirPort Card, it can't take an AirPort Extreme Card. (*Appendix C: Connect without AirPort Adapters* lists some alternatives.)

Figure 1

The AirPort Extreme Card (left) and the AirPort Extreme Base Station (right).

AIRPORT EXPRESS

The AirPort Express Base Station, which started shipping in July 2004, is similar to the AirPort Extreme Base Station, but it supports fewer users and can stream music to your stereo (**Figure 2**).

Figure 2

The AirPort Express Base Station can plug directly into an electrical outlet. Its ports are underneath to allow dangling cables for each kind of media: Ethernet, USB, and audio (from left to right in the photo). The reset button is hidden below.

COMPATIBILITY AMONG DIFFERENT AIRPORT DEVICES

The original AirPort used only 802.11b, but the later AirPort Extreme and AirPort Express both rely on the 802.11g standard. 802.11g is backward compatible with 802.11b, which means that you can mix and match AirPort, AirPort Extreme, and AirPort Express gear on the same network along with any other Wi-Fi-certified B and G gear. However, transfer speeds between pairs of devices running different 802.11 standards decrease to the slower B standard if one device is only capable of B.

For example, an AirPort Extreme Card connects just fine to an original AirPort Base Station, but it uses the slower, 11-Mbps B standard to connect. Likewise, if you try to connect with an original AirPort Card to a G-based AirPort Extreme Base Station, it has no problem: the G base station talks "down" to the AirPort Card at 11 Mbps while still communicating at up to 54 Mbps with G adapters.

NOTE   If you mix B and G devices on a network with a G base station such as AirPort Extreme, the network suffers an overall slowdown because the G base station has to spend more time talking to the slower devices, which reduces the amount of available "air time" to talk at faster rates.

TIP   There's another IEEE standard that's part of some Wi-Fi devices, too, called 802.11a. Where 802.11b and g operate in the 2.4-gigahertz (GHz) part of the electromagnetic spectrum and are compatible with one another, 802.11a uses the 5-GHz band. Because of this, you can't use 802.11a and b/g together. Some manufacturers sell combined a/b/g cards that can use any of the Wi-Fi standards, but you'll be hard pressed to find 802.11a in use.

With the basics out of the way, let's work through picking the best base station for your needs.

SIDEBAR   **OTHER USES OF THE 2.4- AND 5-GHZ BANDS**

Wi-Fi makes use of the fact that the 2.4-GHz and 5-GHz bands are available for unlicensed use: end users require no license or approval to deploy equipment certified by most nations' spectrum regulators. The downside is that *everyone* can use unlicensed equipment without coordination for geography, frequency, or signal strength. All these unlicensed devices have low limits on power, but in an apartment building, office complex, or dense neighborhood, you'll experience interference and see other networks, too.

The 2.4-GHz and 5-GHz bands aren't empty to start with. 2.4 GHz is known as a junk band because it is full of other approved uses that can conflict at times. Industrial sealers, for instance, use heating processes that emit 2.4-GHz radiation. Home microwave ovens employ the principle that water molecules are *dipolar* (have two oppositely charged ends), and these microwave ovens switch the fields 2.45 billion times per second to cause friction which heats the food. (If your friends think microwaves "leak" radiation, create ionizing radiation, or "irradiate" food, please have them read this excellent Q&A page: http://rabi.phys.virginia.edu/HTW//microwave_ovens.html.)

Problems with AirPort networks often stem from your own or neighbors' use of conflicting technology, which can include 2.4-GHz cordless phones, the above-mentioned microwaves ovens, nearby industrial sites, or those horrible X10 wireless cameras. 5 GHz has many fewer approved uses; primarily, 5-GHz cordless phones will be your enemy. AirPort Extreme and AirPort Express have a hardware feature, called Interference Robustness, which can deflect some interference. You can enable Interference Robustness via the AirPort menu for cards and AirPort Admin Utility for base stations; see *Set Interference Robustness* to learn more.

The 2004 Democratic National Convention demonstrated another problem with the 2.4-GHz band: there are licensed users that overlap the 2.4-GHz band and have legal priority, plus they are allowed to shoot out more signal strength. The end result is Wi-Fi being utterly drowned out. At the convention, remote camera crews at the convention were legally using the 2.4-GHz band and destroying Wi-Fi access as they roamed.

Pick a Base Station

"You can paint it any color as long as it's black," is allegedly (but apparently not in actual fact) Henry Ford's statement about choice with the Model T. Apple's similar quotation on Wi-Fi before June 7, 2004, was, "You can have whatever you want as long as it costs $200 or more." Then Apple announced AirPort Express, dropped its AirPort Extreme price, and changed the face of home Wi-Fi.

In this section, you can find out which base station or gateway is right for you. You can find out if the AirPort Extreme or AirPort Express Base Station has particular features you need, and, if not, how an older or alternative gateway could do the trick at a lower price. I'll also review using a Mac as a software base station, making it possible for you to avoid buying a separate piece of hardware altogether.

CONSIDER AN AIRPORT EXTREME OR AIRPORT EXPRESS

Apple has always charged a premium for their AirPort gear because of its ease of use and unique features. That premium was hard to swallow in 2003 and early 2004 when an AirPort Extreme Base Station cost as much as $250, whereas comparable equipment ran for as little as $50 to $80 from companies other than Apple.

In the initial, unreleased draft of this book, I listed many reasons why you shouldn't choose Apple's hardware to build your Wi-Fi network unless you had a few very particular needs. Apple's announcement of the AirPort Express Base Station changed all that, followed by a price drop for their more expensive AirPort Extreme Base Station from $249 to $199. With a price tag of $129, the AirPort Express Base Station has all the features home users need, along with a few extras you can't get anywhere else or at anywhere near the same price, while the $199 AirPort Extreme Base Station isn't a bad bargain if you need features only it provides.

The AirPort Extreme Base Station now comes in two models which, as is Apple's unfortunate wont, have no model numbers. (You can find their part numbers if you hunt.) The AirPort Express Base Station comes in a single model with an extras kit you can purchase separately. AirPort Express replaced the least-featured AirPort Extreme model. **Table 1** explains how to tell them apart.

Table 1: How to Tell Current AirPort Base Stations Apart			
MODEL	**WHAT DISTINGUISHES IT**	**USERS**	**PRICE**

AirPort Express	• Audio jack (controlled via iTunes)
	• Barely larger than a power adapter
	• One Ethernet port
	• Unique client mode for printer sharing/
	  music streaming to any Wi-Fi base station
	• Can't share Internet connection with wired
	  computers
		10	$129

AirPort Extreme (modem)	• Dial-up modem • Antenna jack • Two Ethernet ports • Can share Internet connection with wired and wireless computers	50	$199
AirPort Extreme (plenum)	• Designed for schools and businesses • Plenum rating for fire safety • Power over Ethernet (PoE) • Antenna jack • Two Ethernet ports • Can share Internet connection with wired and wireless computers	50	$249

Commonalities

Important features that the AirPort Express and AirPort Extreme Base Stations share are USB support, AppleTalk support, and wireless bridging. Here's more information:

- **USB support:** All current AirPort base stations have a USB port that allows you to share any of a long list of supported printers among connected Macintosh users with at least Mac OS X 10.2.7 or with Windows users running XP or 2000.

- **AppleTalk:** If you're using older networked printers or Macintoshes, you may need AppleTalk support. Apple's base stations support AppleTalk, of course, but so do some base stations from other manufacturers, including long-time Apple supplier Asanté. Most users have weaned themselves off pure AppleTalk, so this probably isn't a determining factor when you're deciding what to buy.

NOTE Some readers have asked me if the USB port could share a hard drive with a USB interface. For now, the answer is "no": the USB port handles only printers. (Apple states their position on the USB port bluntly at http://docs.info.apple.com/article.html?artnum=107857.)

If you want to connect a USB hard drive to a network, consider the Linksys Network Storage Link (NSLU2). It hooks a USB 1.1 or 2.0 drive—including USB memory drives—to an Ethernet network for $99. Mac OS X 10.2 and 10.3 can connect to it using Samba, as can Linux and Windows (http://www.linksys.com/products/product.asp?grid=35&prid=640).

COOL TIP You can charge your iPod from an AirPort Express's USB port if the iPod is a model that has a Dock and a standard USB cable. The iPod can draw a small charge from the USB port. Thanks for this tip go to Rael Dornfest at Mobilewhack.com (http://mobilewhack.com/).

- **Wireless bridging:** Both the AirPort Extreme and AirPort Express Base Stations support wireless bridging, which allows them to connect to each other without wires to form a larger network. Apple's units are some of a handful of devices that can serve wireless clients while bridging to other base stations. (See *Bridge Wirelessly*.)

Now let's look at the differences.

AirPort Extreme

AirPort Extreme is meant for wireless networks with wired computers and more users than an AirPort Express network. Both AirPort Extreme Base Station models can handle up to a recommended 50 users at a time, and they have robust management tools and built-in features designed to work on complex corporate and academic networks. Never mind that Apple was selling AirPort Extreme models to home users (and still does); AirPort Extreme Base Stations are now more firmly aimed at an audience that needs a bit more and is willing to pay for it.

AirPort Extreme's two Ethernet ports means that you can use a single base station as your link to both a broadband modem via the WAN port and your local Ethernet network via the LAN port.

The AirPort Extreme Base Station with a modem is practically the only Wi-Fi gateway available that includes a modem for connecting to a dial-up Internet connection. If you're using a modem connection and want to use

Wi-Fi at home, this pretty much determines your choice. It can even dial America Online on behalf of individual users—it's the only shared gateway that can handle that. Because it has Ethernet ports, you can easily upgrade to broadband later, too.

NOTE   The modem model of the AirPort Extreme Base Station also lets you call your network remotely using PPP if you set up the base station to answer the phone line. This is handy for some people who have networks that they either can't or don't want to access over the Internet using static addressing or dynamic DNS.

The Plenum/PoE model was designed to be placed in out-of-the-way places, like drop ceilings or within walls or closed compartments. The plenum rating means that the unit meets fire-safety guidelines for off gassing in the event of a conflagration. Power over Ethernet (a.k.a. IEEE 802.3af) pushes DC (direct current) over unused wires in an Ethernet cable, eliminating the need to plug the device into a nearby electrical outlet. (Currently, I can find this model in the Apple Store only if I click the link on the store's home page to view business products.)

Also, AirPort Management Tools 1.0, discussed in *Appendix D: AirPort Management Tools*, enables you to configure several or even hundreds of AirPort Extreme or AirPort Express Base Stations at once, a feature that can save enormous amounts of time in the case of large installations.

AirPort Express

In features, the AirPort Express Base Station is broadly similar to the AirPort Extreme Base Station: it runs at the same speed, but only supports 10 users per base station, whereas AirPort Extreme's recommended maximum is 50 users. AirPort Express has three jacks: the USB printer-sharing port; a single Ethernet port; and an audio-out jack that can handle analog or digital outputs with adapters.

NOTE   *Appendix A: Setting up AirPort Express* contains a full guide to the settings found in the AirPort Express Assistant, explains how to configure an AirPort Express via AirPort Admin Utility, and covers how to use iTunes with AirPort Express.

Ethernet

The single Ethernet port offered by AirPort Express limits you in one important way if you also use wired computers on your network.

You can plug the base station into your cable or DSL modem and share the incoming Internet connection to wirelessly connected computers. But in that situation, you cannot simultaneously share that connection with your wired computers. For such sharing with wired computers, you need at least one separate WAN (wide area network) Ethernet jack, which the broadband modem connects to, and one LAN (local area network) port to hook to an Ethernet hub or switch for wired computers. These ports are offered either by an AirPort Extreme Base Station or a similar device from another maker, which I talk about later.

Audio

The audio jack on the AirPort Express is its truly unique feature. It lets you plug AirPort Express directly into your stereo system and then stream music to it using iTunes 4.6 or later (on Macintosh or Windows) as a controller. For example, if you have an AirPort Express Base Station in the living room, basement, and bedroom, with each connected to a stereo or powered speakers, you can have three separate copies of iTunes that control one set each simultaneously, or one copy of iTunes can select which single set of speakers to control at any given time.

Although you can purchase stand-alone streaming audio adapters that work with Wi-Fi networks, these cost from $125 to $300 and require you to use a different interface—typically a small LCD screen and a remote control—to select and play music.

NOTE   The AirTunes system works on a one-to-one basis: one copy of iTunes can control one set of speakers at a time. You can't stream from iTunes to several sets of speakers at the same time—yet.

Apple sells a $39 AirPort Express Stereo Connection kit that includes both analog and digital optical (Toslink) adapters for its audio plug, along with a separate power cord to make it easier to use the AirPort Express farther from a power outlet. Otherwise, it plugs straight in and hugs the wall (see **Figure 2**, earlier).

TIP   You can purchase a mini-to-Toslink cable from any online audio store for $20 or less, and an analog mini-stereo cable, which connects to the more typical RCA left and right connectors for about $5 from most electronics stores or electronics departments in larger stores.

Modes of network connection

AirPort Express can operate in three modes, among which Apple doesn't clearly delineate, but which I explain as follows:

- **Stand-alone mode:** In stand-alone mode, AirPort Express is just another base station. If it's part of a network that includes other base stations, it connects to the network via Ethernet. If given the same network name as other base stations on the network, clients will roam to it.

- **Wireless network extension:** Using Wireless Distribution System (WDS), the AirPort Express connects to a main AirPort Express or AirPort Extreme Base Station that's connected to the Internet. In this mode, it can extend the network by serving wireless clients, and wired computers through its Ethernet port. (See *Bridge Wirelessly*.)

- **Client mode:** This less-publicized feature turns the AirPort Express into a streaming audio/USB printer adapter for any Wi-Fi network, not just those that have AirPort Extreme or Express Base Stations. The AirPort Express can't handle clients in this mode. It just acts like another Wi-Fi card on the network, in essence. For existing networks, this mode might be useful if you only want the audio and printing features. Apple provides a lot of technical detail about this mode at http://docs.info.apple.com/article.html?artnum=108040.

I describe how to set up each mode in *Appendix A: Setting up AirPort Express.*

DECIDE WHAT TO BUY

Now that you know about the differences between Apple's currently available AirPort models, it's time to determine if you need an AirPort Extreme Base Station, an AirPort Express Base Station, a third-party wireless gateway, a cheap used model, or if you want to go another route entirely with a software base station. If you aren't already clear on which option is right for you, see if one of the following common situations matches yours:

- If you need a modem, a plenum rating, or Power over Ethernet, look to the AirPort Extreme. All these features are uniquely inexpensive (or just plain available) in AirPort Extreme models; other models with these features cost several hundred dollars each.

- If you are seeking a base station for a small or home network with *only* wireless computers, AirPort Express is likely your best choice, but if you don't need USB printer sharing or audio output, you may be able to save about $40 by purchasing a comparable unit from another manufacturer. (Later in this section, I offer specific suggestions for cheaper alternatives from other manufacturers.)

- If your small or home network has wired and wireless computers, AirPort Express with its one Ethernet port won't work on its own as your primary base station, because it can't connect your wired computers to the Internet, so look to AirPort Extreme or a third-party option for the features you need. You can also use additional software and hardware to make AirPort Express work in this scenario, and I explain how later, in *Take Control of Dynamically Assigned Addresses.*

- If you need a secondary base station to extend the range of a wireless network, consider AirPort Express (which offers USB printer sharing and the capability to integrate your music with your stereo wirelessly) or consider cheaper options from other manufacturers (that lack USB and music support).

- If you need a primary base station with a lot of options and want to extend your wireless network's range or features, look to a solution many of my colleagues are switching to: using AirPort Express as an adjunct to AirPort Extreme. Their main base station is AirPort Extreme for its benefits and configurability; the satellites near stereos or remote parts of the house are now AirPort Express for the audio output and lower cost.

- If you want to avoid owning a base station (to save money or so that you don't have to carry it around), you can set up a Mac as a software base station. Typically, the Mac connects to the Internet normally and then uses its AirPort or AirPort Extreme Card to broadcast wireless access to other computers in the area. I talk more about this choice shortly in *Consider a Software Base Station.*

- If you want to save money or consider more options than what Apple offers in the AirPort line, look to gear from other manufacturers, which I discuss shortly in *Consider a Wireless Gateway Alternative.*

TIP   On the client side, it makes the most sense to equip most machines with an AirPort Card or AirPort Extreme Card if that's the only available slot or if you use Bluetooth constantly alongside Wi-Fi. But if you have a Power Mac with a free PCI slot or a PowerBook with an empty PC Card slot, you can shave $30 to $70 off the card cost through alternatives mentioned throughout the book and surveyed fully in *Appendix B: Connect without AirPort Adapters.*

If you decide to buy an AirPort Extreme or AirPort Express, you don't need to read farther in this part of the book. You can skip ahead to *Pick the Right Place for Your Base Station.*

DON'T BUY OLDER AIRPORT BASE STATIONS

If you're keen to stick with Apple at a lower price, you might consider buying a used original AirPort Base Station—but let me talk you out of it:

- **You can't get them cheap:** eBay auctions consistently show completed sales of the graphite and snow models at $60 to $100, which is the same price as or even higher than a new 802.11g, 54 Mbps wireless gateway with a three- or four-port 10/100-Mbps Ethernet switch! The original base station works at just 11 Mbps (802.11b), and the graphite model included only a single Ethernet port, with no extras for connecting any other wired computers.

- **You could get a dud:** Apple had a lot of duds in the early batches of graphite base stations, and to a lesser extent in the snow series. Many graphite units gave up the ghost a year or so into their lives. Apple didn't offer an extended warranty or recall for this well-known problem, and you don't know if the unit you buy might fry. If they were cheaper, perhaps around $35, you could buy two and have a backup. But they're not (yet).

GOOD NEWS! It turns out that there's a simple and relatively inexpensive fix for many dead graphite AirPort Base Stations: replace the capacitor, a piece of circuitry that holds electric charge to regulate flow. Most likely, the capacitor has fried and died.

I used to think you were out of luck if you didn't have the specific expertise or patience to follow online instructions to purchase and replace this part. But there's an easier way. BSRTech.com (http://www.bsrtech.com/) offers the parts and instructions you need to repair this problem for $6.50 plus shipping— if you're handy with a soldering iron.

If you'd rather not melt a lead amalgam on a circuit board, the company will repair it for you for $45, including return shipping, if it's just the capacitor. They can replace other dead parts, too, for additional cost. They buy dead graphite base stations for parts for other repairs, too!

The owner says he's helped with thousands of repairs of these older units, and he says the graphite AirPort Base Station remains a great workhorse with this typical fix. Even better: he's never had to replace a capacitor twice!

- **They lack the faster 802.11g:** You want 802.11g speeds for faster streaming media and sending files among machines on your network. The amount of data you send and receive will only increase, especially as home broadband speeds have started to ratchet up.

- **They aren't as secure:** The original AirPort Base Stations cannot be upgraded to support the two latest security standards, Wi-Fi Protected Access (WPA) and IEEE 802.11i, both of which I discuss in *Secure Your Network*. The only encryption standard that a graphite or snow can handle is Wired Equivalent Privacy (WEP), which is broken, and a determined cracker can gain access to busy networks that rely on WEP.

But, in their favor, graphite base stations will share a connection to wired and wireless machines via a single Ethernet port. As I discuss later, you rarely want to offer dynamic, private Internet addresses on the same Ethernet segment as your broadband connection. But if you have static Internet addresses from your ISP and want to mix dynamic and static addresses on a single network, the graphite is the only AirPort Base Station to offer this feature without complaining. See *Take Control of Dynamically Assigned Addresses*, later, for more on this situation.

Take my advice—move forward and buy a modern wireless gateway, rather than the slower, problematic original models. Those first AirPort models were much loved, but their time has passed.

CONSIDER A SOFTWARE BASE STATION

One the sneakiest ways to save money on a Wi-Fi network is to use software that Apple built into Mac OS 8.6/9.x, and then omitted from Mac OS X 10.0 and 10.1. The software returned in Mac OS X 10.2 Jaguar and continued to improve in Mac OS X 10.3 Panther.

NOTE Mac OS 8.6/9.x calls this feature "Software Base Station," whereas Mac OS X builds it into its more robust "Internet Sharing." I use the term "software base station" or "software access point" to talk about this set of features in any Mac OS or Windows version.

With Mac OS X's Internet Sharing, you connect to a local network, a dial-up service, or a broadband modem using one connection method, like Ethernet, a dial-up modem, or even FireWire daisy-chained to another computer. You then share that connection to one or more other methods of connection.

Mac OS 9's Software Base Station works the same way, but is limited to an Ethernet or dial-up connection being shared over Wi-Fi only instead of the broader Mac OS X options.

In the most typical use, you convert a Mac into your base station, and other computers on the network connect to it just as they would to any regular Wi-Fi gateway. Once you know how to set up a software base station, you can use it on the fly whenever and wherever you need to connect two kinds of networks. For instance, my officemate Jeff Carlson and I used a software base station in a hotel in San Francisco that had free, wired Ethernet connectivity. One of us would hook up via Ethernet and turn on Internet Sharing, and the other would connect over Wi-Fi.

TIP You can do interesting things in Mac OS X with Internet Sharing, such as connecting via Wi-Fi to a base station and then sharing that connection via FireWire. Or, more practically, if you lack a wired Internet feed, you could use Bluetooth or USB to connect to a cellular data connection and then share it via Wi-Fi to a small group.

Although a software base station saves you money and reduces the number of devices you need to manage, you should also consider the drawbacks of a software base station:

- **Range:** The built-in antennas used with AirPort and AirPort Extreme Cards often lack the range of the more advanced or higher-gain antennas found in dedicated base stations.

- **Availability:** Making a Mac into a software access point turns it into something you must monitor and maintain. Stand-alone equipment tends to be more robust than most desktop operating systems, and although even hardware access points can become confused, they require less maintenance and fiddling than the computers that run software access points.

- **Electrical power:** If you're the sort of person who likes to turn off the lights when you leave a room, the extra wattage used by a computer turned on all the time may irritate you. A hardware access point burns from 10–25 watts, while a Macintosh—even with Energy Saver settings set correctly—could run at 150 watts with its monitor turned on. The cost savings is probably minimal, but the principle of not wasting power is what matters. Of course, if you're already running a Macintosh server, turning it into a software base station actually *saves* energy over having another device turned on.

- **Intermittent connectivity:** I don't recommend using a software access point in conjunction with an intermittent dial-up Internet connection, particularly if you want your computers to communicate with one another when you're not connected to the Internet. The reason is that when you're connected to the Internet, your software access point will hand out one set of IP addresses. But when you're not connected to the Internet, your computers will revert to self-assigned IP addresses in the 169.254.0.0 range. This switching of IP addresses is likely to cause irritating problems that go away if you rely on a hardware access point to connect to the Internet and dole out a single set of IP addresses.

NOTE You can bypass this address assignment problem by setting up your own dynamic address server. Flip ahead to *Take Control of Dynamically Assigned Addresses*.

- **Limited encryption:** A software base station can use only WEP (Wired Equivalent Privacy) encryption as an option at this time. This is fine for home use, but a bad idea for business. I discuss WEP's weakness and alternatives in *Secure Your Network*.

NOTE If you want to share files between two wireless computers, you can create an *ad hoc network* and use standard file-sharing tools (see my ebook *Take Control of Sharing Files in Panther* for details). An ad hoc network has no centerpoint, like a base station; instead, computers communicate directly with one another. Under Mac OS X, you can create an ad hoc network by choosing Create Network from the AirPort menu in the menu bar. You enter a name for the network, choose a channel (or let Mac OS X choose it for you), and click Show Options to add a WEP password. You cannot use the more secure WPA encryption with ad hoc networks. When you click OK, your computer becomes an ad hoc node. Other computers can join the ad hoc network by choosing your network from the AirPort menu or similar locations in Mac OS 9, Mac OS X, and under Windows. Ad hoc networks are usually identified with a symbol or other mark to differentiate them from full-blown networks that run through base stations.

I explain how to set up a software base station in *Appendix B: Setting up a Software Base Station*.

CONSIDER A WIRELESS GATEWAY ALTERNATIVE

Depending on the features you need, a $30 to $120 base station from a company other than Apple could fulfill your needs completely. Even compared with the newer, cheaper AirPort Express model, you could still save $50 to $120 by buying from another manufacturer.

I first make a general recommendation if you don't need specific features, and then I move into more specific recommendations for AppleTalk support and for wireless bridging for building a network of more than one access point.

Generic alternatives

It's true that practically any 802.11b or 802.11g Wi-Fi gateway will do. Most of the equipment that's sold by major brands like Linksys, Buffalo, NetGear, and D-Link uses underlying chips, firmware, and even hardware designs from a few chip makers.

If you want the greatest odds of full compatibility and no surprises with Apple's gear, buy a gateway from Belkin, Buffalo, or Linksys. All three companies use the same chips Apple chose for AirPort Extreme, and all three sell inexpensive wireless gateways that include Internet-connection sharing, Ethernet ports, and Web-based configuration, along with full security support for WEP and WPA (see *Secure Your Network*).

For some people, having a three- or four-port Ethernet switch built into a wireless gateway saves the $30 to $50 required for a similar device—an additional savings over the AirPort Extreme and AirPort Express Base Stations.

In particular, you might consider the gateway that has sold more units than any other piece of Wi-Fi equipment, Linksys's solid WRT54G. It costs about $60 from Amazon.com as this book goes to press.

TIP	**UPGRADING FIRMWARE VIA A WEB BROWSER**

If you use gear not made by Apple that requires a Web browser for configuration, you may be unable to upgrade the firmware with a browser running on a Mac. However, before you dig up a PC or leave old firmware on the system, try a few different browsers, including not just Safari and Internet Explorer 5.2, but also less common browsers such as Mozilla, Camino, OmniWeb 5, or Opera. Chances are good that one of them will have the right secret sauce.

Firewalls or JavaScript and Java filters can also prevent proper configuration via a Web browser. If you have difficulties, turn off as much as possible—temporarily—and try again.

AppleTalk

As noted earlier, AppleTalk is the primary stumbling block for most Mac networks: some routers from Buffalo, Belkin, SMC, and Linksys appear to fully handle the older, plain AppleTalk standard used in Mac OS 9 and earlier (and supported in Mac OS X) when sending traffic between your wired and wireless networks.

> **TIP** AppleTalk support can be confusing because most gateways handle all protocols, including AppleTalk, just fine across one kind of network media. So your Wi-Fi segment or your Ethernet segment can see other AppleTalk devices fine. The real problem is routing AppleTalk between Wi-Fi and wired; only a few devices offer that feature.

The Asanté FR1104-G (http://www.asante.com/products/routers/FR1104-G/) seems to be the most Mac-friendly wireless gateway with full support for AppleTalk; it costs about $90 (**Figure 3**).

Figure 3

The Asanté FR1104-G.

> **TIP** If you buy an FR1104-G, make sure that you install the G1.1 firmware upgrade if it didn't ship with the upgrade installed. That upgrade adds WPA security and AppleTalk support, and it was released in April 2004.

Bridging

Many home and small-office networks now take advantage of a feature called Wireless Distribution System (WDS) that's found in most 802.11g gateways, including AirPort Extreme. I explain WDS fully in *Bridge Wirelessly*, but in short, it's an easy way to create a larger network without using Ethernet cables to connect the wireless access points.

The most flexible inexpensive gateway that supports WDS is the AirStation WBR2-G54, which comes from Buffalo. It costs $70 to $90, and it is a full-featured gateway with Ethernet ports (http://www.buffalotech.com/wireless/products/airstation/WBR2G54.html).

It may be possible to use an AirPort Extreme Base Station as your main Internet connection and the Buffalo unit as a remote: I had this working last year when I had Buffalo gateways on loan from the company. Recent reports from users who read my article on the subject on O'Reilly's Wireless DevCenter (http://www.oreillynet.com/pub/a/wireless/2003/08/28/ wireless_bridging.html) said that they saw spotty or no performance after firmware upgrades changed both Buffalo's and Apple's equipment.

802.11b instead of 802.11g

I'm a big proponent of the faster 54-Mbps 802.11g standard because it's more robust and has already dropped to a pretty decent price. But slightly older, 11-Mbps 802.11b-only equipment is incredibly cheap. I've seen new base stations with all the trimmings for $30 or less. Often these are sold with limited-time rebates to help clear out inventory.

If you don't need AppleTalk, bridging, or all the speed of 802.11g, search for bargains or used devices.

Printing

There's no guarantee that a non-Apple gateway that has a parallel or USB jack for a printer can pass print jobs from a Mac unless it specifically promises support for printing from Macs. Windows and Mac OS X have converged somewhat in how they print in recent years, but your mileage may vary.

Cheap adapters

I can't finish this section without explaining how you could save $50 to $100 on a Wi-Fi adapter for your Mac.

If you own an iMac, an iBook, or an eMac, you're stuck: if you want reasonably priced Wi-Fi with reliable performance, buy an AirPort or AirPort Extreme Card, as appropriate to your situation. (Although there are a couple of USB-based Wi-Fi adapters for no-slot models, they tend to cost more than even a used AirPort Card.)

Also, if you use Bluetooth extensively on or near your Macintosh, the AirPort Extreme Card and Apple's Bluetooth adapters coordinate their frequency use. Bluetooth and Wi-Fi both use the 2.4-GHz spectrum band. Mac OS X can coordinate the two wireless technologies so that both work at their highest available speeds. This coordination isn't yet available in any other combination of Bluetooth and Wi-Fi on the Mac.

But if you own a PowerBook or a Power Mac running the latest Apple AirPort software (3.3 or later), or are willing to use a third-party driver, you can typically buy an 802.11b card for $30 or less or an 802.11g card for $50 or less.

I cover the options extensively in *Appendix C: Connect without AirPort Adapters.*

BUY SUBSEQUENT ACCESS POINTS MORE CHEAPLY

A little-known secret to saving money in building a Wi-Fi network is that when you try to cover a larger area and need to use more than one base station, only one of them has to be *smart*. That is, only one needs to have Internet sharing, and PPPoE support built in or turned on, and all the rest of the doodads that let you connect to your ISP.

The other base stations can be dumb. In fact, it's better if they're dumb, because you don't want them also assigning addresss and generally interfering with the Internet-connected gateway. They can also have just a single Ethernet port, like the Linksys WAP54G or WAP11, which are the very definition of dumb but good access points.

So even if you decide that you want to use an AirPort Extreme Base Station as your main unit, you can purchase $50 to $120 access points that have no features except a radio and an Ethernet port, or inexpensive gateways on which you can turn off all the smart features. If you need to hook in a printer or audio output for those other units, that's the time to use the $130 AirPort Express Base Station as a satellite.

TIP	Adam Engst once found a deal on a Uniden 802.11b-based access point such that he paid $33 and got $30 back after a rebate. It's hard to go wrong for $3. Many companies are trying to clear out their inventories of older 802.11b gear, so these rebates aren't uncommon. To find deals like this, subscribe to announcements from http://dealnews.com/.

NOTE	There's nothing wrong with using only AirPort Extreme Base Stations on your network, and some businesses and schools have standardized on them. If you're using multiples of that model, you turn off features like Distribute IP Addresses. You don't use PPPoE or other features; you let these base stations acquire an Internet address via DHCP or assign them a static address on the local network.

It's also true that unless you often move large files around on your network, you might opt for older, cheaper 802.11b gateways as your remotes.

The section *Improve Coverage Area and Range* explains how to connect remote and satellite base stations to a main one in a simple network.

Pick the Right Place for Your Base Station

When you walk around with a cell phone, the number of bars showing signal strength varies with the quality of the signal that the phone can "see." These bars reflect the strength of signals received from nearby cellular network transmitters on towers and roofs. It's the same issue over a much smaller space with a Wi-Fi gateway. Depending on where you place the base station, its signal may or may not penetrate with enough strength to be useful.

First, decide where you want service. Do you want to work in your backyard? Upstairs and downstairs?

Second, think about the obstacles in the places you want to work. Walls, ceiling, floors, and even metal exercise bikes can all absorb and reflect Wi-Fi signals, reducing their range and quality.

Pick a spot that is near the middle of where you want your signal to reach and test to see if it's a good location for your base station. You want to get the best average signal in all the places from which you want to connect. To run the test, just power up the base station: its default settings, no matter what the maker, will provide a name and a signal. If you already have a laptop equipped with Wi-Fi (or can invite a friend with one to help), you can use it as a signal-strength testing device; otherwise, you might use a handheld $30 Wi-Fi detector. (I talk more about these options just ahead.)

> **TIP**   If the spot you want to use is far from your broadband connection or modem line, skip ahead to *Improve Coverage Area and Range* for tips on bringing your connection to your base station or adding base stations to cover more area.

GENERAL TESTING ADVICE

Here are some general tips for finding your ideal location:

*   Leave the base station in one place while you try all the areas you want to use it in.
*   Spend up to 30 seconds in one spot to see if the signal strength varies.
*   Use sticky notes to mark signal strengths at the locations where you work most regularly or would like to spend most of your time. Mark the current location of the base station and the signal strength you're seeing at that location so it's easy to sort out the ideal placement of the base station later.

- When you move the base station, make sure to keep its orientation the same. The antenna in a base station is *omnidirectional*—all directions—but any antenna has better performance in a bubble that parallels its longest vertical side. Putting it vertically on the wall might dramatically change where signals reach.

- If you find you need to put your base station in an odd location for best performance, read *Improve Coverage Area and Range* for tips on locating your base station far away from the rest of your wired network or Internet connection.

NOTE   Both flavors of Wi-Fi have slower speeds for mixed networks or adapters more distant from the central transceiver.

TESTING WITH THE AIRPORT CLIENT UTILITY

If you have Apple's Wi-Fi adapter or any of the compatible cards I talk about later, along with the latest AirPort Software (version 3.4 or later), you can download and install AirPort Management Tools 1.0 (go to http://www.apple.com/support/airport/ and look in the Resources section at the upper right). Once installed, run the AirPort Client Utility and choose your network from the AirPort menu.

This tool is nifty because it provides ongoing monitoring of the signal and transmit rate. The signal (green) and noise (red) lines show how much useful information you're getting. The higher the signal the better, but noise has to remain somewhat below that line for the data on the signal to be filtered out and reconstituted (**Figure 4**).

Figure 4

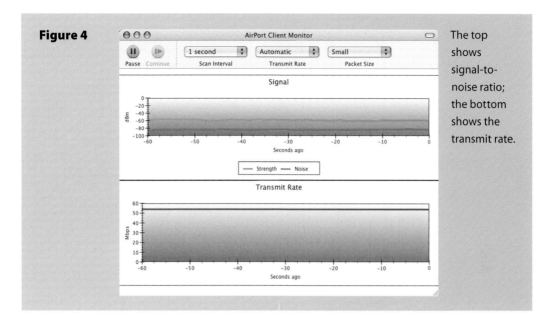

The top shows signal-to-noise ratio; the bottom shows the transmit rate.

The lower half of the tool shows the speed at which your card has connected to the wireless gateway. This is useful to know because you can have decent signal strength but be connected at a lower speed than the 11- or 54-Mbps maximum for 802.11b or 802.11g, respectively.

Testing with other cards

Most other wireless adapters on the Mac have primitive interfaces that lack the monitoring tool support provided with the AirPort family. With other adapters, you're restricted to a signal strength meter, which might show as little information as zero to five bars or dots.

You can also download and install software such as MacStumbler (http://www.macstumbler.com/) or iStumbler (http://www.istumbler.com/). These utilities work with a variety of adapters and can provide more detailed signal strength information plotted over time.

Testing with handheld sniffers

If you'd like to have a laptop-free way to plan a network or if you want to detect more than just Wi-Fi networks, you can use a sniffing device. Wi-Fi sniffers can't tell you anything about the data passing over the network, and they're entirely passive: in other words, they sniff but don't scratch.

Sniffing for Wi-Fi

If you just want to find Wi-Fi networks, you can purchase one of several compact Wi-Fi sniffers that cost about $30 each. These sniffers have a built-in signal detector and use LEDs to display how much signal they can detect in a given area. I recommend a new device, the WiFi Seeker from Chrysalis Development (http://www.wifiseeker.com/). The Seeker is extremely small, quite sensitive, and responds only to Wi-Fi networks (**Figure 5**).

Figure 5

The WiFi Seeker's four LEDs show signal strength of Wi-Fi networks while the button is held down.

NOTE   The WiFi Seeker detects all Wi-Fi networks in the vicinity, so if other networks are operating you can't discriminate which network it's measuring.

Sniffing for more than Wi-Fi

A less Wi-Fi-centric device, the Smart ID WFS-1, shows all 2.4-GHz radiation, including Wi-Fi (http://www.smartid.com.sg/prod01.htm). It can help if you're trying to sort out whether cordless phones, microwaves, or other junk radiation is causing interference problems.

Setting up an Internet Connection

Connecting your base station to the Internet can be as simple as plopping it next to your broadband connection or phone line, powering it on, and making a few configuration changes. Right. And memorizing the capitals of all the states and composing a song about them may be simple, too, but only for those with a particularly odd bent.

What I have found from hard experience is that the little things can make you crazy. To put your wireless network on the Internet, you must use the settings your ISP gave you to get on the Internet with a single computer or a set of computers. In this section, I help you take control of situations that might arise, depending on the kind of connection you make to your ISP.

There are plenty of combinations of options, and it is difficult to anticipate your particular hardware, network, or concerns. To help you make your way through this section successfully, I've put together a flowchart (**Figure 6**). Follow the flowchart to find guidance along your particular path to Internet connectivity.

Figure 6

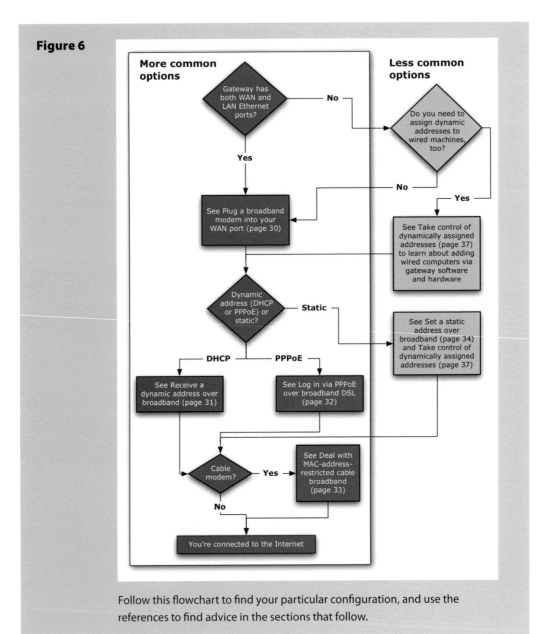

Follow this flowchart to find your particular configuration, and use the references to find advice in the sections that follow.

PLUG A BROADBAND MODEM INTO YOUR WAN PORT

The simplest and best way to put your base station on a broadband network is to connect its WAN (wide area network) Ethernet port to your cable or DSL modem. Then plug any local wired devices (or an Ethernet hub or switch) into the LAN port or ports.

| NOTE | AirPort Express has a single, combined WAN/LAN Ethernet port. I discuss working around this limitation later in *Take Control of Dynamically Assigned Addresses*. |

It used to be a rule that if you connected two devices directly together, you had to use a special crossover Ethernet cable that flipped some of the wires at either end. Fortunately, almost all new equipment comes with a feature called auto-MDI/MDI-X, also known as auto-sensing. This feature enables an Ethernet port to reconfigure itself without intervention for pass-through or crossover purposes. Most WAN ports are either set by default to connect to a broadband modem with a regular Ethernet cable or to have auto-sensing.

RECEIVE A DYNAMIC ADDRESS OVER BROADBAND

Many home users with DSL and cable-modem service are assigned a dynamic IP address via a *DHCP client*. It's called a "dynamic address" because it's assigned to you on the fly, and often changes each time you connect, and sometimes even while you're connected.

The DHCP client requests an Internet address from a DHCP server. The client can run on an individual computer, and some ISPs let you have multiple computers directly connect to their DHCP server. They may charge you a fee for each connected computer. If that's the case, or if your ISP allows only a single DHCP client connection, you can opt to use your gateway's DHCP client to connect to your ISP. In that scenario, your gateway runs a DHCP client on its WAN port, talking to the ISP, and typically runs a DHCP server on its LAN port, to provide addresses to computers on your local network.

Enable your gateway's DHCP client by following your ISP's directions, or, if you lack useful directions, start by using the simplest settings in your configuration software, which you can usually find under an Internet heading as DHCP or Configure Using Dynamic IP.

For example, with an AirPort Extreme or AirPort Express Base Station, you can enable the DHCP client in AirPort Admin Utility by clicking the Internet Connection button and choosing Using DHCP from the Configure menu (**Figure 7**).

Figure 7

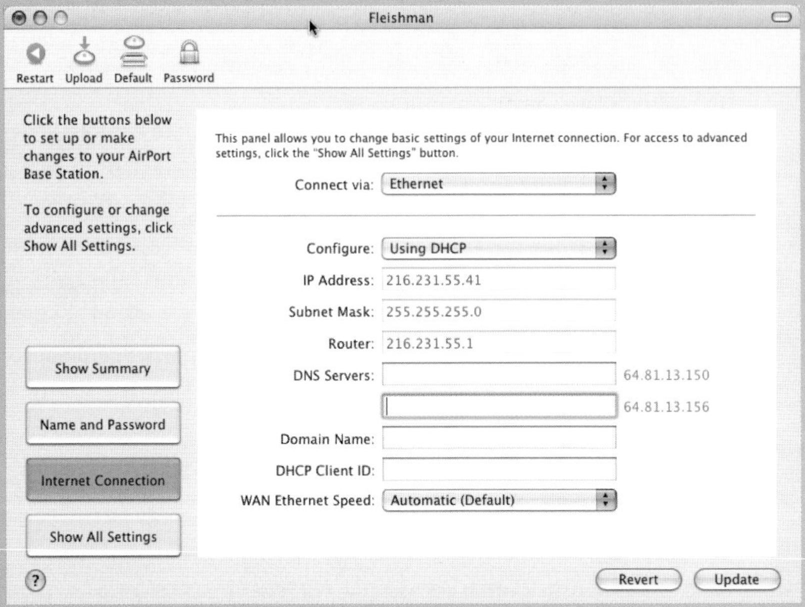

The Using DHCP setting causes the base station to obtain its IP address automatically.

Your gateway may never have the same address twice (or it might hold on to the same IP address for days or weeks; there's no way to predict). However, that shouldn't matter because you almost never need to connect from outside the local network.

NOTE   Do you want to know more about DHCP? Flip ahead to *Take Control of Dynamically Assigned Addresses*.

LOG IN VIA PPPOE OVER BROADBAND DSL

For security and tracking purposes, many DSL providers require you to use a technology called *PPPoE* (PPP over Ethernet) when connecting to their network. With PPPoE, you log in with a user name and password to your ISP over your DSL connection, at which time you are automatically assigned an address and the connection works just like any other broadband connection. If you need PPPoE, configure it in the Internet Connection screen of AirPort Admin Utility (**Figure 8**).

Figure 8

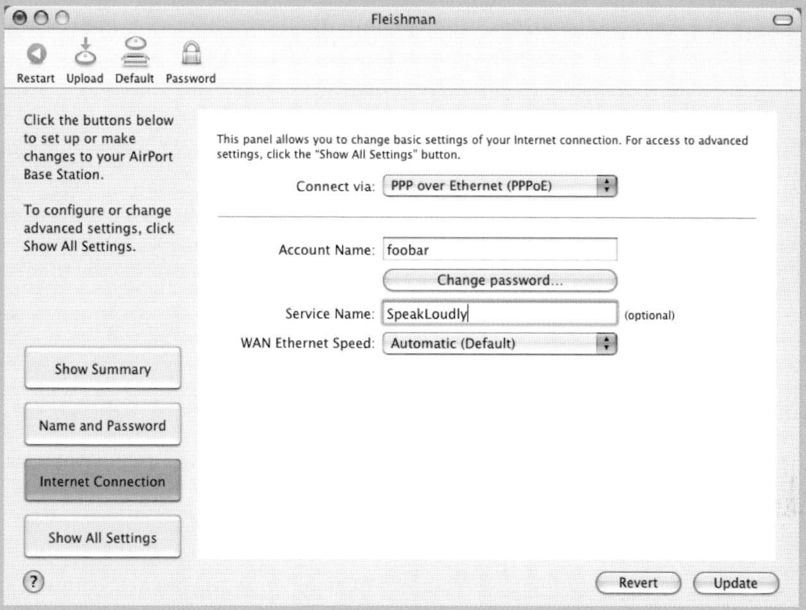

PPP over Ethernet connects using a login name and password.

Virtually all wireless gateways support PPPoE, as it's a routine part of many ISPs' services now.

DEAL WITH MAC-ADDRESS-RESTRICTED CABLE BROADBAND

To prevent multiple machines from accessing a single cable-modem connection, some providers have restricted access to a single *MAC address*, which is a unique number assigned to an Ethernet or Wi-Fi adapter, including individual ports on a switch or gateway. (Find out more about MAC addresses by reading *What and Where Is a MAC Address?* on page 82.)

ISPs use two common methods for restricting access by MAC address. The more annoying method requires you to register your computer's MAC address with the ISP manually or through an automatic installation process; read ahead to find out how to deal with that situation.

The less annoying method involves the cable modem locking on to the MAC address of the device connected to it when the modem powers up. In this case, you can switch between devices (such as a computer and a gateway) simply by powering down the cable modem before you connect the new device.

To work around MAC limitations, most wireless gateways let you extract the MAC address from the one that your cable-modem connection has locked onto and then modify the WAN port MAC address to match it; this is called *cloning.*

WARNING! No release of AirPort base station firmware contains this otherwise common cloning feature, which may make it impossible to share a network connection on a cable-modem service using any Apple gateway.

Typically, the process works as follows, starting with setting up your cable-modem service:

1. Connect your computer to the cable modem and use the software provided by your cable-modem provider to activate your high-speed service.

2. Obtain the MAC address from that computer. (*What and Where Is a MAC Address?* on page 82 explains how to obtain it.)

3. Connect via a Web browser to your wireless gateway.

4. Find the MAC cloning settings, usually found in an Advanced tab.

5. Enter the MAC address and click Update or Restart to apply the setting.

6. Disconnect the computer that set up your cable-modem connection, and plug your wireless gateway into the modem instead.

7. Plug your computers into the wired LAN ports or connect via Wi-Fi to the gateway.

Once you've cloned a MAC address, you can never use that computer and the wireless gateway on the same network segment again. The gateway segregates its WAN port (to the broadband service) and LAN ports (to local wired computers) to avoid MAC-address conflicts.

SET A STATIC ADDRESS OVER BROADBAND

If you arranged with your ISP to obtain one or more static addresses to use with your account, you configure your wireless gateway with what it might call its "manual" or "static" IP settings. Enter the information provided by your ISP exactly, since your ISP's servers won't fill in missing values such as DNS server addresses.

If your ISP provided a range of static addresses that you plan to use on your wireless and/or wired LAN, you can't use your base station as an intermediary between the ISP's network and your own because most base stations won't allow you to assign static addresses—even manually—to machines connected via its LAN port or ports.

You can work around this limitation in three ways:

- The simplest method is counterintuitive. Assign a static address to the base station and then connect it twice to your existing LAN: one Ethernet cable to the gateway's WAN port and one to its LAN port (**Figure 9** shows how you can do this!). By plugging in the unit twice, you allow both static and dynamic addressing from wired and wireless computers on the same network.

WARNING! Some routers may freak out if you try the above workaround—the Linksys wired broadband gateway I tried this with would work intermittently quite well and then stop routing completely until it was rebooted. I eventually had to abandon this strategy.

- Assign a static address to the base station, and connect its WAN port to a switch that contains only computers that have their addresses assigned statically. Any wired machines that need a dynamic address can be directly connected to the gateway's LAN ports or an Ethernet switch connected to its LAN port or ports. Wi-Fi-connected computers will have to receive a shared, dynamic address.

TIP You could set up a second access point with a different network name that had no dynamic assignment built in and attach that to the static side of the LAN described just previously. Connect to that access point if you need to use a static address on your Wi-Fi device!

- Install the gateway with a static address and have it assign addresses to wired and wireless machines via Wi-Fi and its LAN port or ports from a static range of Internet-routable addresses. The AirPort Extreme Base Station offers this option, but many wireless gateways can only assign private, NAT-routed addresses.

Figure 9

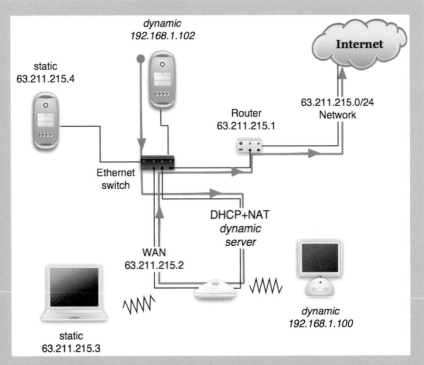

This figure might make your head hurt, but it's simple at heart, and it shows how you can allow a mix of static and dynamic addresses to mingle on a local network of wired and wireless computers:

- The AirPort Extreme Base Station (bottom, center) is providing the dynamic address assignment. Its WAN port has a static address on the local network, and is plugged into the Ethernet switch.

- The base station's LAN port is also plugged into the Ethernet switch, and the base station feeds out dynamic addresses over this port.

Follow the entire red line to see the Power Mac (top, middle) connect to the Internet via dynamic addressing. Its data passes through the Ethernet switch to the base station's LAN port, which repackages it via its static address on the WAN port. The data then goes back to the Ethernet switch, to the router, and out to the Internet.

CONFIGURE A DIAL-UP CONNECTION

If your wireless network connects to an ISP through a dial-up modem, make sure to include alternate phone numbers for the dial-up connection so that you don't have to reconfigure the gateway if one number is often busy.

You may also want to make sure that your base station is set to dial automatically when an Internet service is requested instead of using a manual process, such as connecting via AirPort Admin Utility and clicking a button to dial.

TAKE CONTROL OF DYNAMICALLY ASSIGNED ADDRESSES

Most of us have broadband connections that arrive via a DSL or cable modem. The Ethernet port on these modems is designed, typically, to connect to a single computer. Ha! If you're reading this book, you almost certainly have at least two computers.

All home gateways, whether they have Wi-Fi or not, are designed to work around this. As discussed earlier, gateways typically have a single WAN port to connect to a broadband modem and at least one LAN port for hooking up Ethernet-connected computers or hubs and switches.

Gateways use a combination of Dynamic Host Configuration Protocol (DHCP), the technical name for dynamic Internet address assignment, and Network Address Translation (NAT) to create private addresses and assign them on demand to computers that connect to the LAN through Wi-Fi or Ethernet. Whenever you power up a computer, an address is instantly and automatically assigned to your computer with no involvement on your part—that's DHCP.

DHCP and NAT work together to take the single dynamic address that most ISPs assign each customer and multiply it transparently on your LAN. But there are scenarios in which a gateway's built-in DHCP/NAT combo doesn't cut it:

- If your gateway has only a single Ethernet port, as does the AirPort Express Base Station, you cannot use its Internet sharing because it would pollute your ISP's DHCP service. See *Don't get your service canceled* (page 38) for details and solutions. (In fact, Apple won't let you use an AirPort Express in this manner for this reason; older, single-port graphite AirPort Base Stations allowed it.)

- You want to assign fixed, private addresses to specific computers based on their MAC addresses or DHCP client IDs.

- The limitations of which addresses can be used or other irritations with your gateway mean that you want to configure your own DHCP settings.

- You're running a combination of static and dynamic addresses on one network, and the gateway can't handle both in exactly the way you want it to (as described previously in *Set a Static Address over Broadband*).

Fortunately, you have options. Let's first make sure you don't make your ISP mad by polluting their DHCP service, and then look at four options for dynamically assigning addresses outside a Wi-Fi gateway.

> **TIP**
> There's no good reason to run more than one DHCP server on your network. A single DHCP server that's bridged across wired and wireless networks can provide everything you need, and it ensures that some technologies work properly. For example, it ensures that OpenTalk (née Rendezvous) still connects you to iTunes music libraries (you must be on the same IP network—meaning the same range of addresses—to use this iTunes feature).

Don't get your service canceled

Many ISPs, especially cable-modem providers, bridge your network connection directly onto their network: your Ethernet network is just an extension of their larger pool. This is a stupid design for a variety of reasons, but it's standard practice. (ISPs could use filtering to keep DHCP from leaking upstream, for instance.)

As a result, if you turn on DHCP service on your local Ethernet network and it's not separated by your gateway onto the LAN ports of that gateway, then your DHCP service pushes out to other machines in your ISP's network. When other machines use your DHCP-assigned addresses, they probably won't be able to connect to the Internet at all, and some ISPs will cancel your service in retribution for the trouble you've caused.

If you're assigned a static pool of Internet addresses by your provider and your own subnet mask, then this problem doesn't happen: the DSL modem or digital service router that sits between your network and the ISP won't pass the DHCP service messages. On my office network, for instance, we have a small pool of 64 routable, static IP addresses, and we also run a DHCP service; no conflict there.

If you purchase a single-Ethernet-port base station, like the AirPort Express, then you can feed DHCP and NAT *only* to Wi-Fi clients. The only way around this limitation is to purchase a wired gateway, which I describe shortly, in *Wired broadband gateways*.

NOTE I'm sometimes not so quick on the uptake. While revising this book, I noticed that Apple clearly states in the Network tab of AirPort Admin Utility that the base station being configured is distributing IP addresses via DHCP only to what it labels "AirPort Client Computers," which I interpreted as wireless computers. The technology has worked this way for a long time. I thought, "Huh, did Apple change it so that even an AirPort Extreme Base Station can't provide DHCP service to a wired computer?"

It turns out that the label is misleading. I double-checked what I knew to be previously true, and the AirPort Extreme Base Station *will* feed out DHCP on its LAN port as well as over its Wi-Fi connection. This confusing label is certainly true for AirPort Express, but it is not true for AirPort Extreme.

If you have a LAN and a WAN port on your base station, or don't need to provide access to wired computers, then you don't need to worry about polluting your ISP's DHCP pool.

Configuring DHCP with AirPort

The AirPort Express and AirPort Extreme Base Stations intertwine DHCP and NAT options, making it sometimes difficult to set up precisely what you want. The primary choice depends on whether you want the base station to share an IP address with your entire network by using both DHCP and NAT, or you want it to assign static, routable addresses using only DHCP.

NOTE The screenshots in this book that show AirPort Admin Utility are demonstrating the settings for any AirPort Extreme Base Station. These settings are the same for an AirPort Express Base Station in its stand-alone network mode or WDS mode. The AirPort Express has an additional Music tab that you won't see in the AirPort Extreme screen captures.

DHCP addresses are assigned to all wireless devices that ask to have their address assigned automatically, and similarly to any wired devices connected to network segments that are plugged into the LAN port of the base station.

Follow these instructions to turn on DHCP in your AirPort base station using AirPort Admin Utility 3.4:

1. Run AirPort Admin Utility. (Find it in the Utilities folder, which is inside the Applications folder.)

2. Connect to your AirPort base station.

3. Click Show All Settings.

4. Click the Network tab.

5. Check Distribute IP Addresses (**Figure 10**).

Figure 10

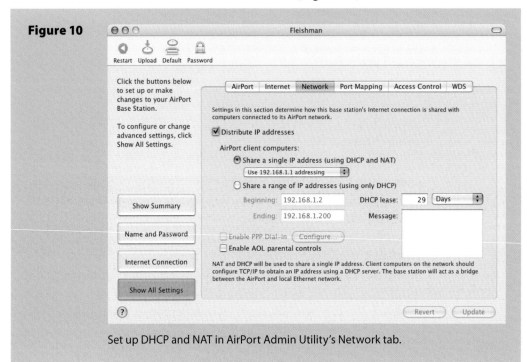

Set up DHCP and NAT in AirPort Admin Utility's Network tab.

6. Set the DHCP lease: a lower number recycles addresses faster; a higher number is better for machines that stay on the network indefinitely. On busy networks, a high lease time can cause you to run out of addresses.

   If your ISP gives you a single IP address that you wish to share with all the computers on your network (the most likely scenario), continue on; otherwise, you're done.

7. Select the Share a Single IP Address (Using DHCP and NAT) radio button.

8. Typically, you can leave the Use 192.168.1.1 Addressing option selected in the pop-up menu, and just click Update.

If you want to switch the private, NAT-generated addresses assigned by the base station, use the pop-up menu to choose one of two other ranges of reserved addresses that don't overlap with real addresses: 10.0.1.1 or 172.16.1.1.

NOTE   Private Internet addresses are non-routable; that is, they can be reached only from other machines on the private network, not from the rest of the Internet— or even the rest of a network that uses a different network range.

The group that assigns Internet numbers reserved several ranges for the purpose of private, local networking. These include 192.168.0.0 to 192.168.255.255, 10.0.0.0 to 10.255.255.255, and 172.16.0.0 to 172.31.255.255.

You can use any of these addresses or ranges within them with 100-percent assurance that no publicly routable Internet-accessible computer has an overlapping address. Of course, computers with these addresses require a gateway running NAT in order to communicate with the rest of the Internet.

You can also choose Other from the pop-up menu to open a dialog where you can define the third number in the IP range (**Figure 11**). You would choose a third number in the IP range other than the default that Apple provides if you were already using the identical network range for some other purpose. For instance, if you already have a network that starts with 192.168.0, you could set your AirPort gateway to feed out addresses that start with 192.168.1. The .1 address, such as 10.0.1.1, is always reserved for the AirPort base station as the gateway address.

Figure 11

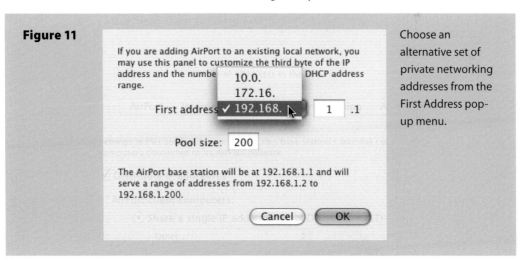

Choose an alternative set of private networking addresses from the First Address pop-up menu.

If you have a range of static addresses provided by an ISP that are fully routable over the Internet, reachable from anywhere, then you can enter all or part of that static range here. If you have a NAT server running elsewhere on your network to map private addresses to one or more public addresses, you can still let your AirPort base station assign IP addresses in that range without running NAT on the base station. Here's how:

1. Working in AirPort Admin Utility's Network tab, select the Share a Range of IP Addresses (Using Only DHCP) radio button.

2. Enter the address range in Beginning and Ending.

3. Click Update to restart the AirPort base station with the new settings.

Configuring DHCP with the Linksys WRT54G

The Linksys WRT54G is designed to run NAT and DHCP as a system quite simply. Here are the steps:

1. Connect to your WRT54G via a Web browser. The basic Setup tab displays by default.

2. In the Network Address Server Settings area, make sure that DHCP Server is set to Enable (**Figure 12**).

Figure 12

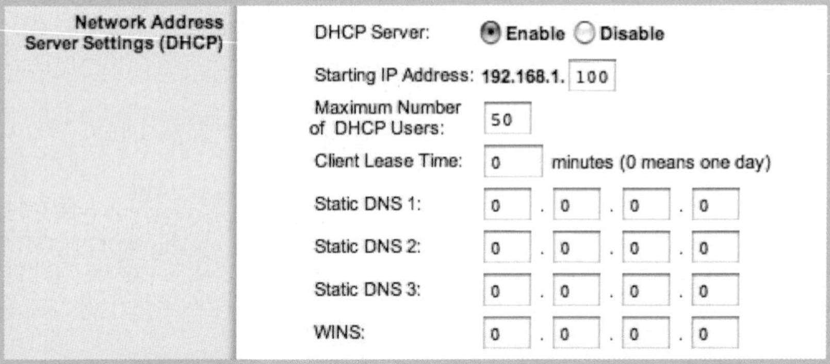

DHCP service is ready to go with just a few entries on the Linksys WRT54G.

3. Set the starting IP address for the DHCP and NAT assignment, as well as the maximum number of DHCP users only if you feel the need to change those values.

TIP   Because the WRT54G acts as an Internet gateway at 192.168.1.1 by default, and since our example here is starting to assign DHCP addresses starting at 192.168.1.100, you can set other machines on the local network to static addresses in the 192.168.1.2 to 192.168.1.99 range by default. For more on this subject, flip ahead a few pages to *Pass Traffic to Individual Computers on a Private Network*.

You can change the first three numbers in Starting IP Address by changing the IP address of the router on the local area network. You change the router's address by entering an IP address in the Router IP fields in the Network tab. You might change the router—and thus the LAN's—private network address if you already are using the Linksys default network 192.168.1.0 elsewhere on the LAN or if you just prefer using a different private network range.

4. Enter the static addresses of the Internet DNS servers that you're using. You may need to ask your ISP for these values. (The WINS setting is needed only for certain kinds of Windows networks.)

5. Click Save Settings to restart the server and enable these changes.

Software-based DHCP servers

Software-based DHCP servers can provide more flexibility or substitute for missing software if you have purchased a gateway that lacks Internet connection-sharing. I've found three software-based methods of adding DHCP and NAT, each of which comes with its own set of advantages and hassles. I provide details in the following pages about each one, but first, here's a quick summary:

• **Panther's Internet Sharing:** I start with the cheapest option (free), looking at the built-in software for sharing an Internet connection within Panther.

• **IPNetRouterX:** This flexible utility from Sustainable Softworks normally costs $100, but you can purchase it for $90 using the coupon at the end of this book. It's a stand-alone software application that provides an interface to Mac OS X's underlying Unix networking services.

• **Mac OS X Server:** This option is the most expensive at $500 or $1000, and it may work only for certain installations. (It has stopped working for me.)

A software-based DHCP server may not be your best choice. You may wish to use a *Wired broadband gateway* instead (page 49). Such a gateway is a fairly cheap and simple-to-configure hardware choice that includes everything you need, avoiding keeping a Macintosh running full-time for just DHCP service.

These software-based DHCP server options work only with a network that uses static IP addresses, or in which a gateway is connected via its LAN ports to the local Ethernet network. If you use any of these methods, you must turn off DHCP and NAT in any existing gateways by unchecking DHCP service or Distribute IP Addresses or similar settings.

Panther's Internet Sharing

Panther lets you run a simple DHCP and NAT server combination through its Internet Sharing feature found in the Internet tab of the Sharing preference pane. Although there are no dialogs for settings, you can still achieve many of the benefits of a more advanced server.

NOTE   Remember that Internet Sharing is Mac OS X's way of creating a software base station, which I describe at length in *Appendix B: Setting up a Software Base Station*.

NOTE   Internet Sharing doesn't support an older method of obtaining an address automatically called *bootp*. It should, but it doesn't. If you have certain kinds of devices that rely on bootp—typically older network appliances, which can include voice-over-IP adapters—then Internet Sharing won't meet your needs.

Follow these steps to set up Internet Sharing:

1. Select the Internet tab in the Sharing preference pane.

2. Choose Built-In Ethernet from the Share Your Connection From pop-up menu (**Figure 13**).

NOTE   Panther lets you share your incoming connection's interface, such as Built-In Ethernet, with other machines on the same interface. Checking Built-In Ethernet in the To Computers Using list spits DHCP service back out on that same wired connection. As noted in *Don't get your service canceled* (page 38), that can be problematic.

            You can also check multiple items in the list of To Computers Using, which means that you can serve dynamic addresses on several interfaces at once. For instance, if you were running a software base station and needed DHCP service on your wired network, you could share the connection from Built-In Ethernet with both AirPort and Built-In Ethernet.

Figure 13

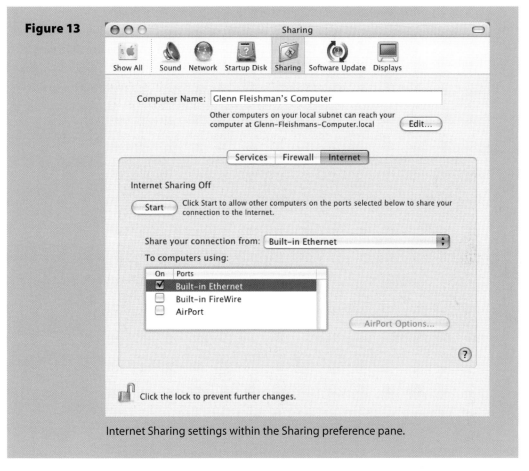

Internet Sharing settings within the Sharing preference pane.

3. In the To Computers Using list, check the Built-In Ethernet box.

    Apple warns you about disrupting your ISP's network (**Figure 14**).

Figure 14

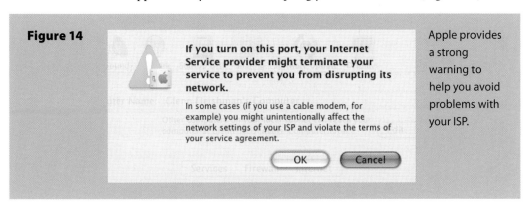

If you turn on this port, your Internet Service provider might terminate your service to prevent you from disrupting its network.

In some cases (if you use a cable modem, for example) you might unintentionally affect the network settings of your ISP and violate the terms of your service agreement.

OK   Cancel

Apple provides a strong warning to help you avoid problems with your ISP.

4. Click OK to close the warning, and then click the Start button in the Sharing preference pane.

IPNetRouterX

If you want to specify exact network ranges and other settings, you can use Sustainable Softworks' $100 IPNetRouterX (http://www.sustworks.com/site/prod_ipnrx_overview.html). (Use the coupon at the end of this book to save $10 on IPNetRouterX.) IPNetRouterX offers a full-featured NAT and DHCP server that also has a behavior-based firewall and sophisticated filters.

Enabling DHCP and NAT in IPNetRouterX is a bit involved, but worthwhile:

1. Open System Preferences, click Network, and from the Show pop-up menu choose Network Port Configurations.

2. Create a new Ethernet network interface by selecting Built-In Ethernet and clicking Duplicate. Name the new interface NAT Interface.

TIP	Your built-in Ethernet interface will be named differently if you have manually renamed it or if someone who set your system up gave it a different name. What you're looking for here is the Ethernet interface that provides your Internet connection.

3. From the Show pop-up menu, choose NAT Interface. In the TCP/IP settings for this new interface, from the Configure IPv4 pop-up menu choose Manually. Set the IP Address to 192.168.2.1 and Subnet Mask to 255.255.255.0. Leave the other fields blank.

4. Click Apply Now.

5. Run IPNetRouterX.

6. Click the Interfaces tab (**Figure 15**).

Figure 15

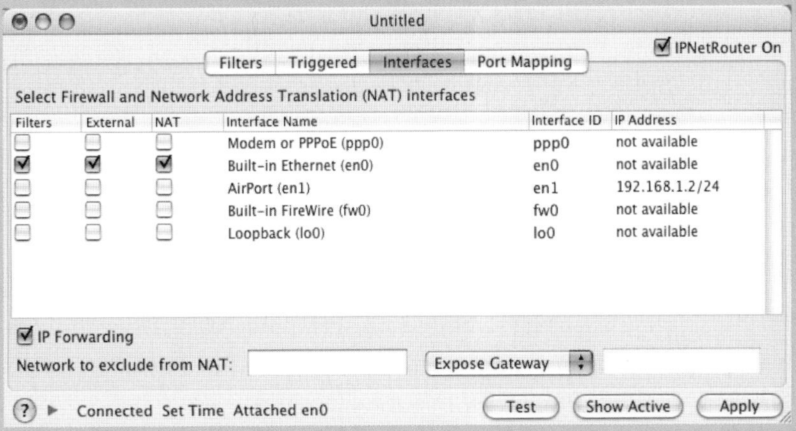

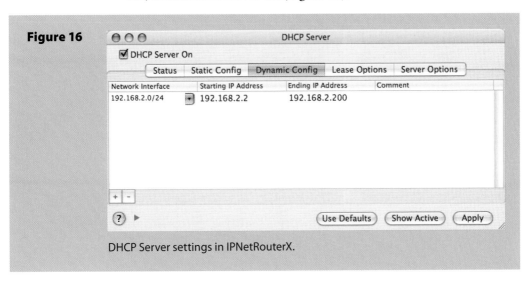

The main settings window for IPNetRouterX.

7. In the upper-right corner, check IPNetRouter On.

8. Examine the row corresponding to the network that is your connection to the Internet; it should have External and NAT checked. The optional Filters checkbox activates IPNetRouterX's rules-based firewall.

9. Click Apply to activate IPNetRouterX with your settings.

10. Choose Tools > DHCP Server and, in the resulting dialog, at the upper left, check DHCP Server On (**Figure 16**).

Figure 16

DHCP Server settings in IPNetRouterX.

11. Click the Dynamic Config tab.

12. Make sure the range of addresses that's provided by default in the 192.168.2.0 network range doesn't conflict with any other service on

your network. You might change the starting and ending addresses to 192.168.2.2 and 192.168.2.200.

13. Click Apply.

14. Choose File > Save to save this configuration.

15. Set this configuration file to load automatically on each restart by adding it to your account's Startup Items list in the Accounts preference pane.

IPNetRouterX has a trick that lets you use it over an Ethernet network in a way that no other method I've discussed allows. The Static Config tab restricts assigning addresses to only those computers that meet criteria. Substitute these two steps for those earlier:

11. Click the Dynamic Config tab, select the default address listed, and click Delete.

12. Click the Static Config tab. Add an entry for each computer on your network using either or both the MAC address and the DHCP Client ID to restrict which machines receive which fixed private addresses.

You can set the DHCP Client ID in Mac OS X by selecting an interface in the Network preference pane, like "DHCP Ethernet" (**Figure 17**), and entering a unique client identifier (anything you want) in the DHCP Client ID field. The MAC address is found in the Ethernet tab for Ethernet interfaces, and in the AirPort tab for the AirPort adapter. (See *What and Where Is a MAC Address?* on page 82.)

NOTE   During my research for this book, IPNetRouter X's developer, Peter Sichel, said via email that when you assign fixed IP addresses in this manner, his DHCP server is entirely quiet until it hears an appropriate request from a machine with the right credentials.

Figure 17

The DHCP Client ID can be used with Static Config in IPNetRouterX to assign the same address to a computer every time it's on the network.

Mac OS X Server

If you're already running Mac OS X Server 10.3 for some other reason, you can also have it act as a DHCP and NAT server. The configuration is quite complicated, unfortunately, requiring changes in the DHCP, NAT, and Firewall services. I've written a long article about this for the O'Reilly Network, and it is available free online at http://www.oreillynet.com/pub/a/wireless/2003/11/25/nat_panther.html.

WARNING!

After writing version 1.0 of this text, I found my Mac OS X Server setup had failed, and I was unable to restore it through many hours of effort. In Apple.com's forums and elsewhere, I discovered equally frustrated Mac OS X Server users. I wound up switching to a software gateway.

Although Mac OS X Server has many powerful features, it lacks good error reporting that lets you troubleshoot the problems between its friendly graphical interface and the underlying configuration files. Several people have written to me with the same problem I've encountered and the same frustration.

Wired broadband gateways

It's easy to overlook this last option, yet it's a cheap and simple method to add DHCP service to your network. While most broadband gateways are sold with Wi-Fi as a full wireless option, you can still purchase inexpensive hardware boxes that have all or most of the same features but no Wi-Fi. These devices are the ideal solution when you're trying to use a single-port base station, such as the AirPort Express, with wired computers on the same network.

Take a look at the Linksys BEFSR41, for instance, which has a street price of about $50. On the LAN side, it's a four-port 10/100 Mbps Ethernet switch with automatic cable-type sensing—no uplink ports, in other words. Its WAN port runs at 10 or 100 Mbps, too, and handles all the major ISP login types.

PASS TRAFFIC TO INDIVIDUAL COMPUTERS ON A PRIVATE NETWORK

Most gateways come with primitive firewalls that often comprise nothing more than NAT: because NAT hides computers from the public Internet, it's a passive firewall. Others come with more powerful active firewalls that can detect whether or not a real attack is being attempted and temporarily or permanently block that attacker.

But with either passive or active firewalls, you may find yourself stymied if you have any software servers, like a Web server, on your local, private network that you want to have others connect to from the public Internet. This is also an issue if you play Internet-enabled multi-player games that require two-way access, as each side acts like a mini-server for the other side.

Many non-Apple Wi-Fi and wired gateways include a feature known as *Universal Plug and Play,* abbreviated UPnP. If this feature is turned on in the gateway, as it often is by default, programs running on Windows computers on your local network signal the gateway that they want two-way communications, and the gateway seamlessly sets this up (**Figure 18**).

Figure 18

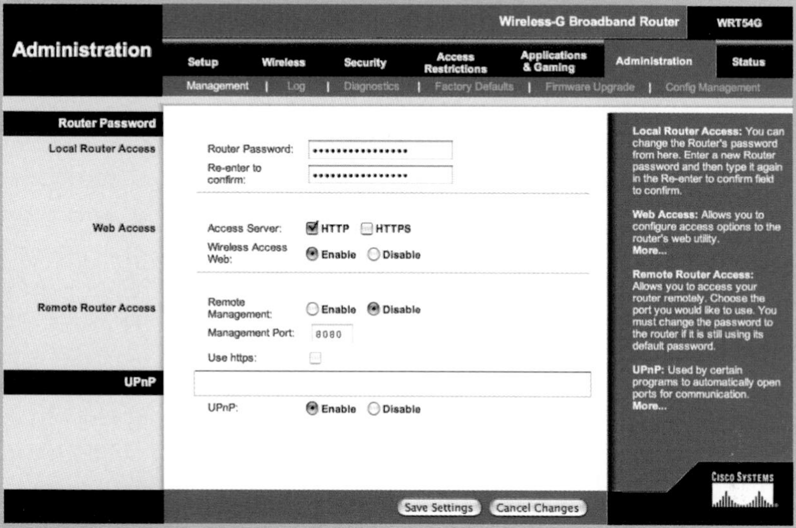

The UPnP setting is at the bottom of this configuration screen for a WRT54G. Enable it for programs to open up ports automatically.

Because Apple doesn't support UPnP in either Mac OS X or its AirPort gateways, if you use any AirPort base station or if you have Macintoshes on your network that need to get through a UPnP-supporting firewall, you must employ a more tedious method of punching through the firewall for Macs. To do so, you need to know about ports.

Ports

Every kind of server you might run, including a personal Web server and your side of a game transaction, uses a *port* to communicate with the rest of the machine, network, or world. A port in Internet networking can be compared to an apartment number in a typical postal mail addressing system: a computer has an IP address just like an apartment building has a street address, and each kind of service used by a computer has a port number, just like each apartment has its own number within the building.

With ports, it's as if every apartment building had the manager in unit 1, the mailroom in unit 25, a lounge in unit 80, and so forth. Ports are consistent for the same services on whatever machines those services are running on.

Taking it one step further, if you only have static addresses, that's like having a street-front address. NAT-provided private addresses are like buildings within a gated compound.

So how do we punch through this gate that wisely surrounds our network? You use features called *port mapping, port triggering,* or *DMZ host.* If you have an AirPort, you are limited to port mapping. However, if you run a gateway from practically any other manufacturer, you can choose your technique based on the programs and services you use.

WARNING!   Anything you do to punch through ports or computers from the private network to the outside world reduces your security. Be careful about what you leave open. You may want to provide better security on computers that you expose in this fashion by installing active firewall and intrusion-monitoring software.

Port mapping

When you map a port, you make the gateway connect one of its Internet-accessible ports to the same (or a different) port on a computer on the otherwise-private inside network.

The gateway listens for traffic on the specific port on its public, WAN interface. When a connection needs to be opened, it reroutes the traffic from that public interface port to the appropriate private address on its LAN interface, whether that's a Wi-Fi LAN or a wired LAN (**Figure 19**).

The following pages have step-by-step instructions for how to set up port mapping in an AirPort Express or Extreme Base Station and in the popular Linksys WRT54G network.

Your first big step is to get around a limitation in how these devices handle port mapping if you use DHCP and NAT. You can set a static private address for each computer that needs to be mapped outward. After that, you can configure your particular Wi-Fi gateway for port mapping.

Figure 19

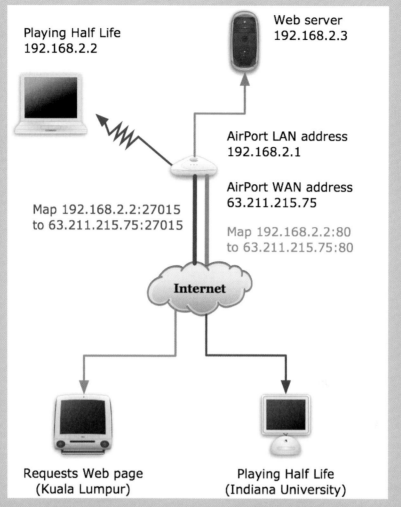

One user on a laptop is playing Half Life over the Internet; another computer on the network is running a Web server. When a user in Kuala Lumpur requests a Web page, the gateway maps the incoming request on port 80, the standard port for Web servers, from its public address to the Web server's private address. Likewise, when traffic needs to run over port 27015, the standard port for Half Life, the gateway connects traffic from a player at Indiana University with our network's laptop user.

Setting a static, private address for port mapping

Both Apple and Linksys require that you enter a static address to set up port mapping for each port or range of ports you want to map from the outside world to your little neighborhood. But if you're using NAT and DHCP to assign addresses to the machines on your internal network, they may end up with different dynamically assigned addresses on occasion, even if you set the DHCP lease time to years or decades. Machines reboot; gateways reboot; they don't always assign the same number to the same computer.

The way around this is to ensure that you reserve a chunk of the address space that DHCP would otherwise assign dynamically. You can then manually assign addresses in that chunk to machines that are running servers or playing games. Once those machines have static IP addresses, you can map ports to them from the outside. Here's how to reserve the address space:

• **In AirPort Admin Utility:** Connect to your base station, and click the Network tab. With Distribute IP Addresses checked, choose Other from the menu below Share a Single IP Address (Using DHCP and NAT). You can set the pool size, which is the number of addresses assigned out starting at a given address. IP addresses in the range .201–.254 (shown in **Figure 20**) are then available for manual assignment.

Figure 20

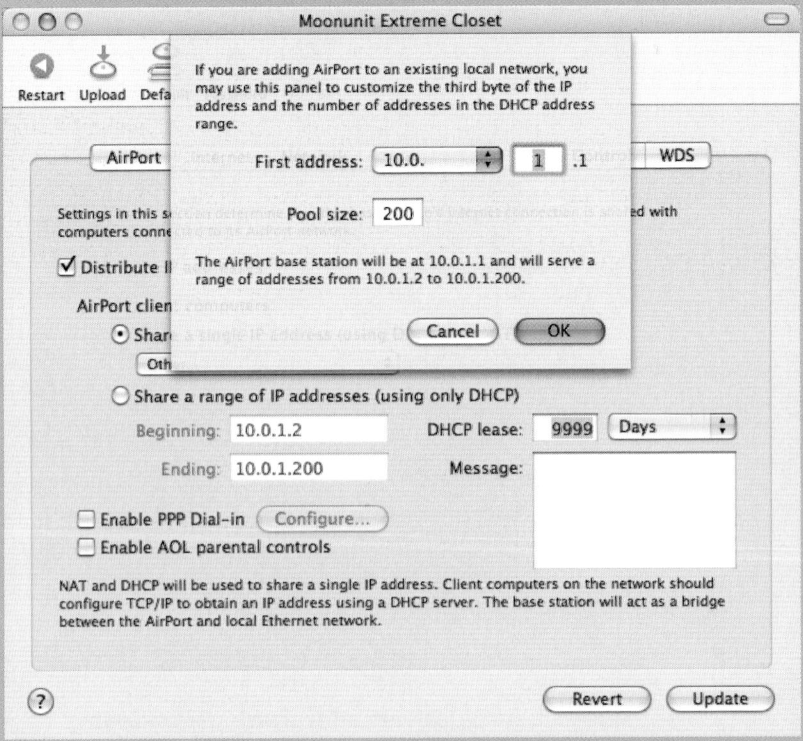

Using the Other menu to set DHCP pool size in AirPort Admin Utility.

- **On a Linksys WRT54G:** In the Setup tab's Network Address Server Settings (DHCP), you can set DHCP Server to Enable, choose a starting IP Address for the range of addresses it assigns, and choose the Maximum Number of DHCP Users (**Figure 21**). In this instance, the DHCP pool runs from .100 through .149; you can manually assign addresses from .2 to .99 and from .150 through .254.

Figure 21

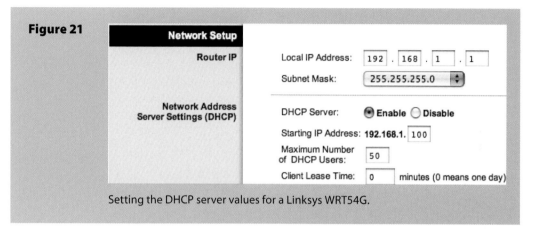

Setting the DHCP server values for a Linksys WRT54G.

In both cases, the gateway uses the address ending in .1, the addresses in the pool may be assigned dynamically to computers by the DHCP server, and you can manually assign addresses in the range outside the pool to specific computers you want to use with port mapping.

That's the gateway side of the equation, but now you must configure each computer so that it can use one of these static addresses. Instead of letting the computer pick up an IP address via DHCP, you must:

- Manually assign an address from the available range, like 10.0.1.201 in the AirPort example earlier, or 192.168.1.2 in the Linksys example.

- Apply a subnet mask of 255.255.255.0

- Set the router to 10.0.1.1 (AirPort example) or 192.168.1.1 (Linksys example).

- Obtain and enter the domain name server values.

A computer configured manually like this can still access the Internet: the gateway's NAT server still translates between the internal and external IP addresses. But what's important is that the internal IP address won't change over time, which makes it possible to use it with port mapping.

Set port mapping with AirPort Extreme or AirPort Express

You can apply port-mapping settings with an AirPort Express only when it is set to use WDS or to create its own network. In client mode, you rely on the wireless network it's connecting to. AirPort Extreme can always set port mapping. Here are the steps:

1. Run AirPort Admin Utility and connect to your base station.

2. Click the Port Mapping tab. (In AirPort Admin Utility 3.4 and earlier, click Show All Settings to reveal this tab.)

3. Click Add to display a dialog into which you can enter port-mapping details (**Figure 22**).

Figure 22

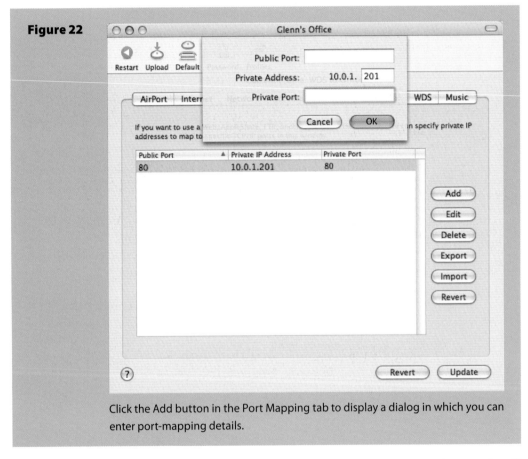

Click the Add button in the Port Mapping tab to display a dialog in which you can enter port-mapping details.

4. In the Public Port field, enter the port that computers on the outside will connect to on the gateway. This is often the same port number on the local network.

5. In the Private IP Address field, enter the network number that corresponds to the computer on the local network.

6. In the Private Port field, enter the internal computer's port number.

7. Click OK to record your settings.

8. Click Update to update the AirPort base station's settings.

Repeat steps 3–7 as necessary for all the ports you want to map. Unfortunately, Apple does not let you enter port ranges, a tedious missing piece for programs that require more than just a few open ports.

Set port mapping on a Linksys WRT54G

The Linksys WRT54G has a broader range of options that are easier to set for port mapping, which it calls *port forwarding*. It also allows port triggering and DMZ, which I describe next.

1. Bring up the Linksys configuration screen via your Web browser.

2. Click the Applications & Gaming tab (**Figure 23**).

Figure 23

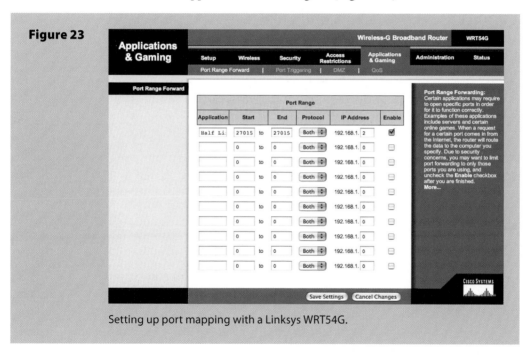

Setting up port mapping with a Linksys WRT54G.

3. Enter a descriptive name in the first Application field.

4. Enter the Start and End port numbers that need to be accessible from the outside in their respective fields. If you're mapping only a single port, enter its number in both the Start and End fields.

5. Choose UDP or TCP or Both, depending on what's needed, from the Protocol pop-up menu. If you're uncertain, leave Both selected.

6. Enter the static IP address's last digit in the IP Address field.

7. Check Enable.

8. Repeat steps 3–7 on the next available row for each service you want to add.

9. Click Save Settings to reboot the server and enable your new settings.

Linksys doesn't let you map public ports to different private ones. This is generally not a problem, but it would prevent you, for instance, from mapping the external port 80 to port 8080 on an internal computer.

Port triggering

Port triggering is similar to port mapping, but it requires a "tickle" from the outside world to get started. Port triggering is often used by games or chat programs. When the gateway receives a request on a certain port or range of ports, the gateway then—and only then— opens a different set of ports. It's a tool used to restrict access and to leave ports otherwise closed.

The AirPort models don't support port triggering, but you can configure port triggering in the Linksys WRT54G using the Port Triggering tab under its Applications & Gaming tab (**Figure 24**).

Figure 24

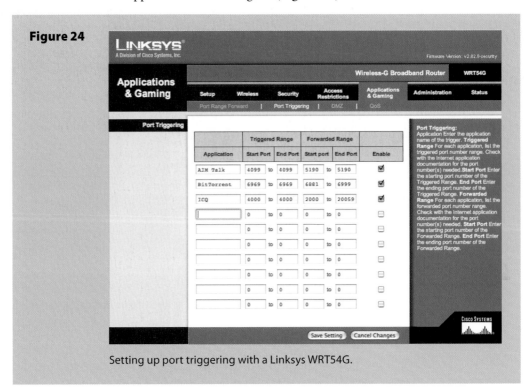

Setting up port triggering with a Linksys WRT54G.

With port triggering, you enter a name in the Application field, a range of triggering ports, and a range of forwarding (or mapping) ports. Check Enable to turn them on. Click Save Setting to apply changes and restart the router.

DMZ host

The final method of passing traffic through a NAT gateway is DMZ, which exposes all the ports on a single computer on your internal network to the outside world. DMZ is a horrible misuse of the term "demilitarized zone": turning it on puts the exposed computer firmly over the border into enemy territory, i.e., the wide open Internet.

Apple doesn't offer a DMZ option, but Linksys does. Here's how to turn it on: In the Applications & Gaming tab, click the DMZ tab (**Figure 25**). Then, enter the last digit of the private IP address that you want to expose to the outside Internet and click Save Settings to update the router and reboot it.

Figure 25

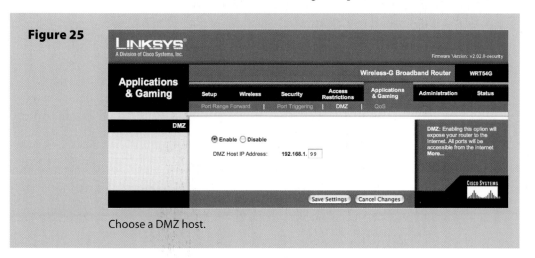

Choose a DMZ host.

Setting up a Shared USB Printer

In this section, I explain how to set up and print to a printer connected to the USB port on an AirPort Express or AirPort Extreme Base Station. Before you start with any of the specific steps, make sure your printer is supported by Apple. They support a huge range of devices, but if yours isn't on the list, you're out of luck until they add support. You can find the list at http://docs.info.apple.com/article.html?artnum=107418.

If your printer is in the list, plug it into the base station and turn it on. You should not need to reboot your base station for it to recognize the printer. Now you're ready to configure your machines to print. I provide directions for configuring recent Macintoshes (below) and Windows XP machines (shortly).

ADD A SHARED USB PRINTER IN MAC OS X 10.2 AND 10.3

1. Open your printer utility from the /Applications/Utilities folder. In 10.2, it's Print Center. In 10.3, it's Printer Setup Utility.

2. Click Add.

3. Select Rendezvous from the topmost pop-up menu. (This choice may change to OpenTalk in future releases as Apple retires the Rendezvous name.)

4. Find your printer in the resulting list and select it, and then click Add.

Your printer should appear in the list, and you should be able to print to it. However, if your printer doesn't show up, try the suggestions offered just ahead.

NOTE   You can also add a printer from the Print dialog. From the Printer pop-up menu, either choose Edit Printer List or choose the printer from the Shared Printers submenu, if it's there. After you add the printer, it shows up in the list of printers in the Print dialog's Print pop-up menu and can be used like any locally connected printer.

Don't choose the printer from the Shared Printers submenu again, or you may create yet another instance of the printer!

TROUBLESHOOT AN UNAVAILABLE SHARED USB PRINTER

If your shared USB printer doesn't appear in the pop-up list of printers in a Print dialog box under Mac OS X or under Windows XP, one of the following suggestions should shed light on the problem.

- Make certain that the printer is powered up and not in an error condition (such as out of paper or out of ink).

- Make sure your computer is on the same network as the base station (make sure you can see the base station via AirPort Admin Utility).

- Make certain the base station recognizes the printer. In AirPort Admin Utility, connect to the base station. If there's a powered-up, supported printer attached, its name and model number will appear next to USB Printer when you select Summary from the View menu.

- Restart the base station via AirPort Admin Utility and try again.

- Double-check that your printer appears on Apple's list of base-station-compatible printers. If your specific model is not included, you are likely out of luck until Apple adds support (http://docs.info.apple.com/article.html?artnum=107418).

ADD A SHARED USB PRINTER IN WINDOWS XP

The following advice comes in general form from Mac OS X Hints (http://www.macosxhints.com/), a great Web site for technical advice. I was initially stymied in my attempt to convince my Windows XP box to print to a shared USB printer, and the advice on Mac OS X Hints was of great help in getting started. Here are the steps:

1. Open Printers and Faxes from the Control Panel.

2. From Printer Tasks in the list of tasks in the left navigation bar, click Add a Printer.

3. The Add Printer Wizard appears. Click Next.

4. Select Local Printer Attached to This Computer. Uncheck Automatically Detect and Install My Plug and Play Printer. Click Next.

5. Select Create a New Port (near the bottom of the screen). Choose Standard TCP/IP Port from the pop-up menu, and click Next to launch the Add Standard TCP/IP Printer Port Wizard. Click Next again to show the Add Port screen.

6. For Printer Name or IP Address, enter your base station's private network address, which might be 192.168.1.1. You can find this address

by seeing what the gateway address is in Network preferences under TCP/IP. Leave Port Name alone; Windows will fill it in for you. Click Next.

7. On the next screen, choose Hewlett Packard Jet Direct from the pop-up menu next to the Standard radio button. I don't know why, but Mac OS X Hints found that it works. We obey. Click Next.

8. Click Finish to return to the first wizard. From the list of manufacturers and printers, select your precise model. Click Next.

9. The final screen has you name your printer. By default, it uses the name from the model type in the previous screen. You can enter a new name if you'd like to, however. Select whether or not you want this printer to be your default by clicking the Yes or No radio button. Click Next.

10. Leave the Do Not Share This Printer radio button selected unless you want to share the printer. To share it, click the Share Name radio button and enter a name. Click Next.

11. Choose to print a test page by leaving the Yes radio button selected, which is the default, and click Next.

12. Finally, click Finish.

Walk over to your printer and see if a test page was printed. If so, you're ready to go. If not, check through the steps to make sure you configured everything correctly or try the suggestions on the previous page.

Improve Coverage Area and Range

The top question I receive about Wi-Fi is, "How can I extend the area served by my Wi-Fi network?" Several strategies let you cover more of your home or business without having to spend a fortune—$50 to $200 could double to quadruple your coverage area.

ADD ADDITIONAL ACCESS POINTS FOR ROAMING

A relatively simple way to extend a network is to add access points. As noted earlier in *Buy Subsequent Access Points More Cheaply*, you want additional access points to be *dumb*. They should lack features like providing DHCP service or have them turned off. Only your main access point should be *smart*, "firewalling" the outside world, connecting to the ISP, and handling other Internet and security tasks.

When you add additional access points, they must have the same network name, known as an *ESSID* (extended service set identifier). This enables computers to move around without changing their network settings because their AirPort cards automatically and seamlessly switch from one access point to another as needed to maintain a constant connection to the network. If you have encryption enabled, each access point must have the same options and keys set.

A very small number of wireless gateways don't permit roaming: Asanté had one 802.11b model, for instance, that didn't allow it, which surprised me. But all the 802.11g gateways from major manufacturers that I know about do allow roaming.

When adding access points to create a network that allows roaming, you need a network backbone that connects all the access points. Typically, you use Ethernet cabling to connect the access points (**Figure 26**). However, you can also use wireless connections or electrical connections to form that network backbone, as I describe in *Bridge Wirelessly* and *Extend with HomePlug*.

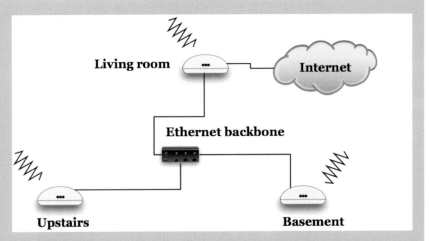

Figure 26

A simple network topology with one base station connected to the Internet in the living room; another base station upstairs; and a third in the basement. They're all connected by Ethernet to a switch.

The most important part of adding access points is choosing the Wi-Fi channels for them wisely. Wi-Fi has 11 overlapping channels in the U.S.; some countries have as many as 14, such as France. For best performance, you should use the channels that are most distant from one another in the same physical area at the same time: channels 1, 6, and 11 (U.S.) or 1, 7 or 8, and 14 (other countries).

TIP The important thing is to avoid overlapping channels, so if you have only two access points, for instance, you could make them channels 1 and 6, or you could set them to 2 and 10—the details don't matter as long as they're far enough apart.

You might consider using 802.11b access points to extend an 802.11g network unless you really need the speed everywhere. Often, an 802.11g base station has more advanced features or is easier to configure, making it worthwhile as your main hub, but potentially overpriced for outlying base stations.

TIP Although there's no problem with mixing 802.11b access points with an 802.11g base station, do note that your fastest extended network comes from using all 802.11g-capable devices connected to Ethernet.

SIDEBAR   **LIGHT UP WITH POWER OVER ETHERNET (POE)**

It's relatively easy to pull Ethernet cable to remote locations, but running extension cords for power is more difficult. Power over Ethernet, or PoE, is an interesting way to position access points in areas where it's hard, expensive, or dangerous to bring electrical power. PoE used to be too expensive for all but institutional use, but it's come down in price.

With PoE, the Ethernet cable that brings the network to the wireless gateway also brings power at a low voltage over the copper Ethernet wires. This works because Ethernet is DC (direct current) electricity modulated in a certain manner, so running straight voltage is a small step. A PoE network needs power injectors on both ends that separate juice and data, or just on one end if you use a wireless gateway such as the AirPort Extreme Plenum model. Only a few Ethernet switches include PoE in each port and can be configured port by port to inject power into the cable. These are mostly expensive switches, but the feature should catch on over time.

PoE is most often used for exterior applications, like putting a base station in a rugged, weatherproof case on the roof of a house or building. An Ethernet cable carrying 12 volts at low amperage is much safer than the full 110- or 220-volt equivalent of a real outlet.

For beginners, your best bet is a kit from Macwireless.com, which sells several configurations for AirPort base stations (http://www.macwireless.com/html/products/poe/). HyperLink Technologies offers a more extensive but more technical set of PoE adapters (http://www.hyperlinktech.com/web/poe.php).

Don't run standard Ethernet cable outside unless you enclose it in conduit! The plastic shielding isn't designed to resist ultraviolet light or water, and it will likely break down within 6 months. Although it's more expensive and harder to work with, you need Ethernet cable rated for outdoor use, or even for direct burial. Ask at electrical supply stores or electronics stores. Some cable has a gel around the insulated wires inside a wrapper to avoid cracking during a freeze.

Also, look into proper grounding. You don't want lightning to destroy every device on your network or burn down your building. If in *any* doubt, consult a qualified electrician.

BRIDGE WIRELESSLY

Wireless Distribution Service (WDS) is a neat way to extend an AirPort network without running wires between locations. As I noted previously, if you want to extend a network by adding access points, you might connect them via Ethernet—which means using more wires. Instead, WDS can connect an access point to other access points as easily as wireless clients connect to an access point.

How it works

WDS works in a manner very similar to plugging an Ethernet hub into an Ethernet switch. An Ethernet hub interconnects all the connected devices to each other as a single segment, just like wireless clients connecting to a wireless base station. An Ethernet switch, by contrast, isolates each port as a separate segment. A computer connected to a hub connected to a switch's port can reach computers on other ports' hubs because the switch knows to transfer data across segments based on where the computers are located.

Likewise, WDS allows access points to exchange information about where computers and other devices are located on a physical network. One access point can then route data to another or to a series of other access points to reach the destination computer (**Figure 27**).

Figure 27

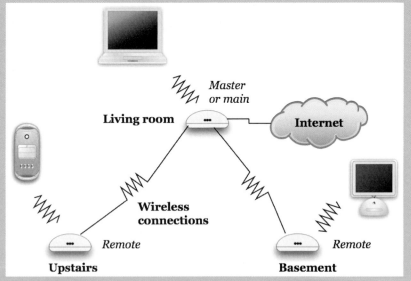

The same basic setup used for an Ethernet-connected network can work with WDS. Here, each base station is set to WDS and to serve access to local computers wirelessly as well.

NOTE The biggest downside in WDS is that on a busy network, you effectively halve, quarter, or even eighth, your available bandwidth: all the network traffic that travels among access points over WDS reduces the overall throughput of the network. But with an effective network throughput of about 25 Mbps on an 802.11g network, even splitting that into pieces still provides plenty of usable bandwidth.

WDS options in hardware

Unfortunately, WDS appears in different forms in each wireless gateway that includes it. The best implementations come from Apple and Buffalo Technology because these companies' base stations allow a base station to work as an access point serving access to local wireless clients while simultaneously connecting to one or more base stations to exchange data across a wireless backbone.

In general, to set up WDS you need to know the MAC address for each of the wireless gateways you want to connect (see *What and Where Is a MAC Address?* on page 82). However, the AirPort Extreme Base Station will scan for other gateways, letting you simply select them by name.

Apple, Buffalo, and Linksys each have distinct approaches to how they allow WDS to be used. WDS suffers from a not-so-theoretical issue called the "hidden node" problem, which is exacerbated or mitigated depending on the approach.

Apple's WDS approach

Apple considers one device the master, which they call a main base station. This device is usually the one best positioned to connect to an Internet feed. Base stations that connect to the main are called remotes, and they relay traffic via the main to and from their clients, whether to other clients on the local network or out to the Internet. Finally, Apple defined a relay, which a remote can connect to and which is in turn connected to a main. You could have 4 remotes on each relay and 4 relays connected to a main for a total of 21 base stations (**Figure 28**), although bandwidth would be enormously reduced.

Figure 28

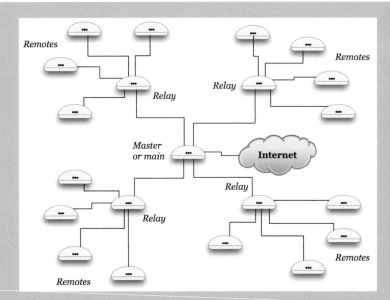

If one main base station tells four friends, and they tell four friends…well, this is what happens.

SIDEBAR

THE HIDDEN NODE PROBLEM

In a mesh network in which multiple wireless access points connect to each other, the "hidden node" problem occurs when one node has at least two access points that can see the node but can't see each other. Because Wi-Fi works very much like Ethernet, it relies on collision detection that requires that every device on a segment can spot when other devices start transmitting and then back off.

With a hidden node, some devices can't tell when other devices are transmitting, resulting in crosstalk, interference, and other problems. When designing a network to use WDS with more than a few points, you may have to give this issue some consideration. In some cases, you'll see a performance reduction if you ignore it; in others, the network might mysteriously vary in its quality and reliability.

TIP

AirPort Express can function only as a main, a remote, or a relay, just like AirPort Extreme. AirTunes—streaming music from iTunes to a stereo through AirPort Express—works just fine over WDS. See *Appendix A: Setting up AirPort Express.*

Buffalo's WDS approach

Buffalo allows each base station to connect to up to six others. They don't all have to connect to one another, either, resulting in complicated topologies that might not always work because of the hidden node problem. Simpler is better.

Linksys's WDS approach

Linksys decided to allow its WAP54G access points (not gateways) to be only in WDS-bridging mode or in access-point mode. As a result, you would have to buy two Linksys wireless access points to have both the benefit of wireless bridging and to service local client computers. Although that scenario doubles your cost, you can set the bridges to an entirely different Wi-Fi channel, which essentially doubles your overall network throughput.

Configuring WDS on an AirPort Extreme or AirPort Express Base Station

The modern AirPort base stations are designed to hook more easily to one another via WDS. You can even bypass some of the configuration steps by using the AirPort Express Assistant to enable WDS on one of those base station models. Here's how to set up WDS:

NOTE One important limitation of using Apple's version of WDS with AirPort Extreme or AirPort Express: you can't use the more powerful WPA encryption to protect the network's traffic. See *Protect More Easily with WPA* for more details.

1. Open the Applications folder, then the Utilities folder, and run AirPort Admin Utility 3.4.

2. Choose the base station that you are setting as the main base station from the left pane and connect to it.

3. Click Show All Settings and click the WDS tab (**Figure 29**).

4. Check Enable This Base Station as a WDS, and choose Main Base Station from the pop-up menu.

5. If you want this unit to act just as a bridge, uncheck Allow Wireless Clients on This Base Station.

Figure 29

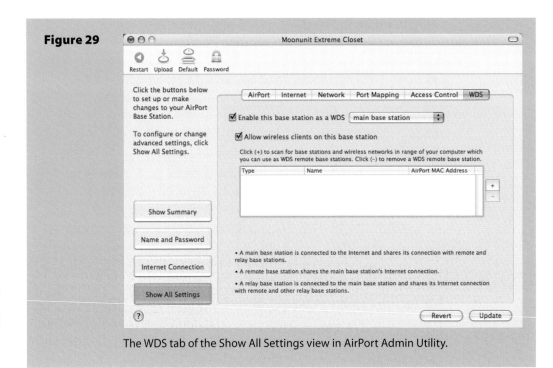

The WDS tab of the Show All Settings view in AirPort Admin Utility.

6. Click the + (plus) button to the right of the empty list box in order to see a dialog that lists other base stations (**Figure 30**).

7. Select the base stations you want to add one at a time. Leave Auto Configure as a WDS Remote Base Station selected to skip connecting to the remote base station and configuring it through these steps as well—the software on the main base station handles that for you.

8. I recommend testing each base station as you add it by clicking Update in the main Admin Utility screen, waiting for the base station to reboot, and then making sure clients can connect (if enabled) and bridge on all attached units.

9. Repeat steps 1–8 for each additional manually configured remote base station and for every relay base station.

Configuring WDS on a Buffalo gateway

This configuration works for all 802.11g Buffalo gateways with WDS. My example uses the WLA2-G54 base station.

Figure 30

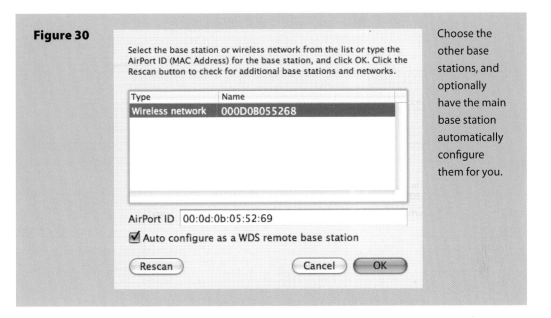

Choose the other base stations, and optionally have the main base station automatically configure them for you.

1. In the Web configuration screen of one bridge in the WDS set, click the LAN Setting option in the left navigation bar, and then click Wireless Bridge (WDS) below it (**Figure 31**).

Figure 31

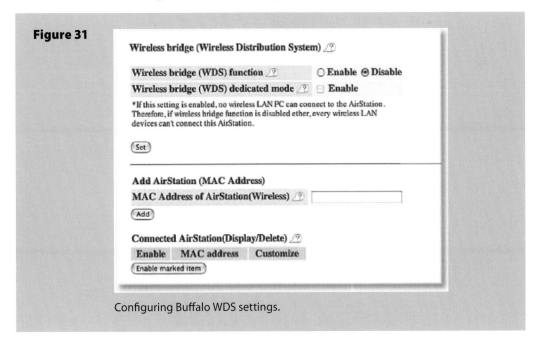

Configuring Buffalo WDS settings.

2. Select the Enable radio button next to Wireless Bridge (WDS) Function.

3. If you want the unit to act just as a bridge and to not serve local wireless clients, check the Enable box next to Wireless Bridge (WDS) Dedicated Mode.

4. Click Set, and then return to this page after the unit reboots.

5. Enter the MAC address of the first unit in its colon form (00:00:00:00:00:00) and click Add. You may have to reboot the gateway, although that shouldn't be necessary.

6. Repeat steps 1–5 for a complementary unit to the one you just configured.

7. Test that the two work together and are carrying traffic. If they are, then repeat steps 1–5 for each additional unit. Each unit should contain the MAC address for each other unit that's part of the same WDS set.

EXTEND WITH HOMEPLUG

What's the most robust and ubiquitous wired network in your home? The electrical system! We don't think of data transmitting over power, but all wired networks use electricity to encode data. In the case of HomePlug— sometimes known as Powerline—small adapters plugged into outlets modulate data over the 60-hertz (Hz) cycle used in U.S. power. It's not the fastest network you'll see, offering a real throughput of about 6 Mbps, but that's about what you'll see from 802.11b, and likely not much different from a network extended with WDS.

HomePlug has no central hub in most cases. Macintosh users should purchase $50 HomePlug Ethernet bridges, which offer a single Ethernet jack. You plug a cable from your Mac into this bridge, and you're done. The HomePlug system handles communication among all the adapters on your electrical network.

To extend a wireless network, simply place your access points in appropriate locations, give them the same network name, set them to non-overlapping channels, and then plug them into HomePlug Ethernet bridges (**Figure 32**). And that's it.

Figure 32

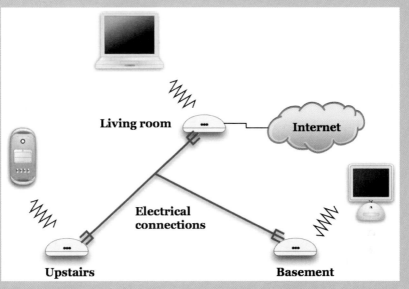

HomePlug connects via the electrical wiring in your home using one Ethernet bridge per access point.

TIP   You can enable robust encryption on the HomePlug network—it uses 56-bit DES—but you almost always need a Windows system to run the configuration software unless you purchase a pair of MacWireless.com's $80 bridges that come with Mac software (http://www.macwireless.com/html/products/powerline/). Unless you're in an apartment building or other shared area in which you're concerned about people tapping in to your network via HomePlug, don't worry about it.

There's an interesting option for HomePlug and Wi-Fi: one form of HomePlug bridge is a wireless access point of the dumb variety, exactly the kind I recommend. For about $80, this HomePlug Wi-Fi adapter can be the compact extension to your network that you need.

ADD AN ANTENNA

If you can't reach every part of the area you want, the temptation is to boost the signal. Adding an antenna can increase the range of your Wi-Fi gateway, but it's not necessarily the best choice.

Because Wi-Fi is a two-way transmission, just boosting the point's power and sensitivity doesn't necessarily mean that a client will magically work better. In many cases, adding a second inexpensive access point will offer superior advantages with less monkeying around (and in fact, Wi-Fi was designed around adding access points to extend range).

The fundamental problem with adding antennas is that it's technically illegal in many cases in the U.S. and elsewhere. In the U.S., the FCC doesn't require users of Wi-Fi equipment to have licenses; Wi-Fi operates in *unlicensed* bands. But the FCC does require every device that uses these bands to be tested and certified by them to assure that it conforms to standards.

Despite the fact that many wireless gateways come with antennas that can be removed or with jacks to add antennas, it's still not *de facto* legal to just swap in any old antenna you buy. It's perfectly legal to *buy* antennas with the right connectors, but *deploying* them is another matter because the FCC wants to preserve the airwaves and human health. Poorly chosen antennas with high gains could exceed legal limits and could even endanger someone.

The FCC has recently loosened restrictions, so which antennas you can add legally depends on when and how the equipment was certified:

* **Before July 2004:** Any Wi-Fi equipment that was certified by the FCC before this point can be used only with antennas that were tested and approved with that device. You cannot have an FCC-approved antenna that's legal with any of these gateways; you can only have an FCC-approved system that includes an antenna. There has never been a charge or arrest for this widespread activity, but I can't legally recommend it.

* **Beginning July 2004:** The FCC changed the rules to allow manufacturers to test high-gain antennas of each major type (omnidirectional, for instance) that produce the maximum legal signal strength. Once tested, the manufacturer can ship a device with any antenna of equal or lower signal strength. Users can also exchange the shipping antenna (if any) with an antenna up to the maximum gain tested. Equipment certified in this fashion allows you the maximum legal flexibility.

You can purchase antennas legally from several companies; HyperLink Technologies (http://www.hyperlinktech.com/), QuickerTek (http://www. quickertek.com/), and MacWireless.com (http://www.macwireless.com/) sell a variety of antennas, including ones designed specifically to work with AirPort and AirPort Extreme Base Stations and Linksys gateways.

Antennas come in several varieties, but the most useful antenna for general purposes is *omnidirectional,* which means it can send signals in all directions.

SOLVE THE TITANIUM POWERBOOK RANGE PROBLEM

If there's one subject I've heard way too much about, it's the terrible range of the AirPort Card in the Titanium PowerBook G4. The poor range is caused primarily by the poor placement of the antenna in the base rather than in the screen.

Even though the Titanium PowerBook G4 has been replaced with the better-performing aluminum 15-inch PowerBook G4, there are hundreds of thousands of Titanium PowerBook G4s floating around, and many still-frustrated users who aren't ready to replace their machines.

Several suggestions have been made over the years to improve the Titanium PowerBook G4's range, but the simplest and most effective is to remove the AirPort Card (you can sell it on eBay for a decent price, amazingly enough) and add a third-party 802.11g PC Card from Linksys, Buffalo, or Belkin. Some people particularly like the Sony PCWA-C150S because it matches the titanium finish of the PowerBook G4 and doesn't stick out far.

As long as you're running Mac OS X 10.2.8 or later and AirPort 3.1.1 or later, you can simply plug in the replacement card, and the AirPort software treats it like a built-in device. With a PC Card, you'll enjoy terrific range because the card moves the antenna entirely outside the laptop's case.

You can also opt for a USB adapter or a variety of other older, cheaper cards or higher-powered cards, which I talk about in *Appendix C: Connect without AirPort Adapters*.

SET INTERFERENCE ROBUSTNESS

Why not use a setting labeled Interference Robustness to more robustly resist interference and thus improve range? In short, it won't help with range but it might provide a more reliable connection over a short distance.

Apple offers Interference Robustness as a setting for the AirPort Extreme Card, AirPort Extreme Base Station, and AirPort Express. Apple describes the option sketchily on their Web site, saying that it provides better performance in the presence of 2.4-GHz cordless phones and near working microwave ovens, both of which produce noise in the same spectrum band used by AirPort and Wi-Fi (802.11b and 802.11g).

Unfortunately, Apple hasn't provided more information, and the option doesn't seem to make much difference in normal networks. One Web site documents testing that indicated that the setting increases power while reducing reception sensitivity, thus blasting through the interference when sending data, while listening less carefully (ignoring more noise) when receiving it.

Turning Interference Robustness on is helpful only if you use Wi-Fi at a short distance from a base station and if you believe that interference is the culprit. Interference Robustness reduces the range, but can improve performance within that smaller range.

Better than using Interference Robustness, if you operate 2.4-GHz cordless phones, you might consider switching to older 900-MHz phones (lower quality but often better range) or newer 5.8-GHz phones (higher price, and range is an issue).

Turn Interference Robustness on for an AirPort Extreme Card through the AirPort menu in the menu bar: choose Use Interference Robustness. For an AirPort Extreme or AirPort Express Base Station, set this option in AirPort Admin Utility. In the AirPort tab, click Wireless Options, and then check Enable Interference Robustness.

TALK TO YOUR NEIGHBORS

A frustrating part of Wi-Fi networking is that you can't control your "air space." All too often, neighboring Wi-Fi networks cause reception problems in areas that otherwise would have good reception. If your network's performance varies by time of day or even minute to minute, these ideas may help you identify the problem:

Do some basic testing:

- Investigate your 2.4-GHz cordless phone and microwave oven as culprits—they can both put static on the Wi-Fi line; see *Set Interference Robustness*.

- Run MacStumbler (http://www.macstumbler.com/) or iStumbler (http://www.istumbler.com/) to determine whether other networks are running in the vicinity. These two programs each scan for networks and can identify characteristics about them, such as signal strength and whether security is enabled.

If a neighboring network is causing the problem:

- Be aware that the so-called "108" or "Turbo G" technology made by Atheros is especially problematic. The gear works at its highest speeds only with equipment by the same maker, and some testing has shown that Atheros's technology can dramatically reduce the speed of nearby

Wi-Fi networks using any channel and any other makers' chips. Those results aren't definitive, but it's a good place to start if you're trying to diagnose a problem.

- If your neighbor is using Turbo G equipment typically made by NetGear or D-Link, ask them to download and install firmware upgrades that offer a dynamic version of the proprietary speed boost. This dynamic version scans for competing networks and backs off a bit if it might impact a network.

- Propose an informal channel usage agreement: if your neighbor and you are both using channel 6, switch to 1 and 11 to increase the distance between signals.

- You (and your neighbor) could also consider moving your access points farther away from one another to reduce the signal strength conflict in the middle.

TIP   Another way to reduce network overlap is to engage in unilateral or multilateral curtailment (you know, like the former Soviet Union and the United States). You can cut the amount of transmit power on many Wi-Fi gateways, which reduces the interference you cause. If your neighbor backs off a little, too, both sets of network improve. You know: the Prisoner's Dilemma.

To reduce transmit power from an AirPort Express or AirPort Extreme Base Station, run AirPort Admin Utility, connect to the base station, and click Wireless Options in the AirPort tab. Set Transmitter Power to a level below 100 percent, click OK, click Update, and then re-test.

Secure Your Network

If you use a wired network in your home, someone would have to break into your house, plug into your Ethernet switch, and then crouch there in the dark to capture data passing over your network.

Wireless networks have no such protection: anyone with an antenna sensitive enough to pick up your radio signals can eavesdrop on all the traffic passing over your network. This could be a neighbor, someone parked in a car, or a nearby business. Many free, easy-to-use software packages make this a simple task for only slightly sophisticated snoopers.

However, you're not powerless to prevent such behavior. Depending on what you want to protect and whom you're protecting against, you can close security holes with tools that range from a few settings up to industrial-grade protection that requires separate servers elsewhere on the Internet.

But before I delve into the details of protecting yourself from snoopers, let's look at whether you even need to turn on security.

LIKELIHOOD, LIABILITY, AND LOST OPPORTUNITY

When Adam Engst and I were writing *The Wireless Networking Starter Kit, Second Edition*, we had a disagreement over how much security concern the average home Wi-Fi networker should have. Adam came up with a great formulation that I agreed with and want to walk you through. He calls it the three L's of security: likelihood, liability, and lost opportunity. This framework lets you evaluate how much security—if any—you need to apply to your network.

Likelihood

The first aspect of security to consider is likelihood: how likely is it that someone will violate your privacy, steal your data, or otherwise exploit you? If you live in a lightly populated area, and no one could easily come within range of your network without sitting in your driveway, you probably don't have much to worry about.

But if you live in an apartment building with neighbors who could pick up your connection, the likelihood of someone connecting to your network rises significantly, generating the question of whether you want to allow others to share your Internet connection or not.

The likelihood of attack increases significantly if you're running a business, since it's plausible that your network would carry sensitive information such as credit card numbers, business plans, and so on. Also, most businesses are located in areas or buildings where someone could easily sit and hack into your network without being noticed.

Liability

What is the realistic liability if someone were to record all the traffic that passed across your wireless network? For most home networks, the amount of network data that's at all sensitive is extremely low; perhaps a credit card number being sent to a unusual Web site that doesn't use *SSL* (Secure Sockets Layer, a security standard for Web servers), maybe financial data, possibly some bits that would be embarrassing if made public.

Simply allowing someone else to use your Internet connection has a relatively low liability in most cases. However, you may think differently if you pay per byte, if you have a slow dial-up connection that would be impacted by someone else's use (with high speed DSL and cable modem connections, you're unlikely to notice another user), or if you're concerned that allowing someone else to use your connection would be violating your ISP's terms of service in a way that was likely to result in you being disconnected.

Businesses are, once again, a different story. The likelihood of sensitive and confidential information passing through a business's wireless network is much higher, of course, and the liability of an outsider learning that information is significantly greater. If a business's customer data were extracted from a wireless network, it could involve a disastrous loss of reputation and even lawsuits. And if a competitor learned confidential business plans, the ramifications could be catastrophic.

Lost opportunity

With home wireless networks, the opportunity cost for layering on security comes mostly in the form of troubleshooting irritating problems, which is more necessary and harder when security is on, and in the annoyance of dealing with passwords with new machines or when you have visitors.

Companies, even small ones, may have fewer lost opportunities because they might have a dedicated staffer or whole department that deals with installing, maintaining, and supporting the software that allows overall security.

Your spot in the security spectrum

It's up to you to determine the likelihood of someone breaking into your network and either using your Internet connection or eavesdropping on the data that flies by. Next, you must determine the severity of the problems that would ensue from someone using your bandwidth or using a network sniffer to record your data. Lastly, you need to figure out what the lost opportunity of different levels of security is: the higher the likelihood of attack and the higher the liability if your network were to be invaded, the more you're probably willing to spend and the more annoyance you're willing to endure.

Once you've worked through those three thought exercises, you can determine just how much money and effort you should expend to secure your wireless network. Now let's look at how you might apply such security precautions.

SIMPLE TRICKS THAT DON'T WORK

You may have read suggestions for setting up basic security that advise you to hide your network's name and make it hard to connect to. These techniques are called *closed network* and *MAC address filtering*.

Closed network

In a closed network, your base station stops broadcasting its network name or SSID (Service Set Identifier) as part of its *beacon*, an "I'm here" message that access points regularly transmit in order to help clients connect to them. However, the beacon continues to be sent because it still includes information that is used for network data synchronization.

An open network appears by name in the AirPort menu or in other places in the Mac OS that show the name of networks you can connect to. But closing the network makes it only slightly obscure. A cracker knows the network exists, and by simply monitoring for a connection or causing a temporary outage and a computer's reconnection, the cracker can grab the network's name. So you cannot rely on closing your network for any real security.

TIP	Joining a closed network through the AirPort or similar interfaces just requires knowing its name. With an AirPort adapter, choose Other from the AirPort menu and enter the network's name precisely as you set it or as it was provided to you.

TIP	If you close a network, you can't use the AirPort Express Assistant to connect via WDS to an existing AirPort network. You have to employ AirPort Admin Utility instead. See *Appendix A: Setting up AirPort Express*.

MAC address filtering

MAC address filtering sounds more promising initially. With this method, you enter the MAC address of every computer you want to allow to connect to your Wi-Fi network. If a computer's address isn't in the list, then it can't connect.

On the AirPort Extreme Base Station, for instance, you use AirPort Admin Utility to connect to the base station and, via the Access Control tab, add the MAC address of each computer (**Figure 33**). (*What and Where Is a MAC Address?* on page 82 explains how to find adapters' MAC addresses.)

Figure 33

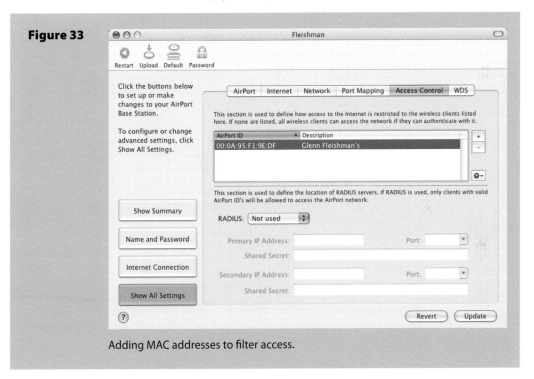

Adding MAC addresses to filter access.

The flaw with MAC address filtering is that any cracker worth her salt can easily monitor a network to see which MAC addresses are able to access the network. She can then use simple software to modify or *clone* the MAC address on her own network adapter to use one of those addresses, thus gaining access.

TIP   If you use MAC address filtering and your network has multiple base stations, each one must have the same list of allowed MAC addresses.

Although MAC address filtering and a closed network will deter casual passers-by, they don't really constitute a defense. You can step up security through the methods described next.

SIDEBAR   **WHAT AND WHERE IS A MAC ADDRESS?**

The *MAC*, or *Media Access Control,* address has nothing to do with Macintosh computers. Instead, it represents a unique address for every network device, including Ethernet and Wi-Fi adapters. A MAC address consists of six two-digit hexadecimal numbers separated by colons, such as 0C:F2:33:01:02:FC. The first three pairs of numbers are assigned to a manufacturer; Apple has at least two common ranges, which begin with 00:0a:95 and 00:03:93.

Because MAC addresses are now so frequently used for filtering, authentication, and WDS, the numbers are easier to find. Buffalo and Apple print the MAC address of the WAN Ethernet port and the Wi-Fi adapter on the back or underside of their hardware.

You can also find these numbers through the admin program or Web interface you use to configure a wireless gateway. For any AirPort gateway, run AirPort Admin Utility (found in /Applications/Utilities). Select the base station from the left pane, and the MAC numbers show up at the right. The AirPort ID is the device's wireless MAC address.

Apple prints the MAC address of their AirPort equipment on the underside of the base station, too. There's a label that has the MAC address for the WAN port, LAN port (if any), and AirPort ID for its Wi-Fi adapter. The last six digits of the AirPort ID form part of the default network name when you power up an AirPort gateway for the first time, like "AirPort Network 003396".

To find the MAC address of an AirPort or AirPort Extreme Card, open the Network preference pane in System Preferences and choose AirPort from the Show pop-up menu. The MAC number is listed as the AirPort ID. (Ethernet MAC addresses are labeled as Ethernet ID in the Ethernet adapter's settings in the Ethernet tab.)

PROTECT WITH WEP

From 1999 to 2003, the only straightforward way to secure a wireless network was by using *WEP* (Wired Equivalent Privacy). WEP is a system that enables you to invent an encryption key and enter it on a base station and all connected adapters. This key is used as the basis of encrypting all data that passes over the network. Without the key, the data appears to be gibberish.

The reason to turn WEP encryption on is twofold: first, to make sure that only people with the key can join and use the network; second, to obscure the traffic you're sending so that it remains private.

If neither of those issues is a concern, you can skip WEP and WPA in the next section. But most home Wi-Fi networkers feel safer with at least a little protection.

WEP basics

WEP comes in two key lengths: 40 bits and 104 bits; longer keys were seen as more secure, and hardware that uses them once cost more. WEP keys are generally entered as hexadecimal or base-16 numbers. A 40-bit WEP key is 10 hexadecimal digits; a 104-bit WEP key is 26 hexadecimal digits.

NOTE Because 16 bits of a WEP key aren't unique, you can also see WEP keys described as 64 and 128 bits—occasionally, even incorrectly as 56 bits. But that's just terminology—the basic keys are 40- and 104-bits long; the extra 24 bits that are sometimes included are a counter that helps increase randomness.

Some gateways let you enter 5 or 13 text characters to create the short and long WEP key through simple mapping. These sets of characters are called *ASCII WEP keys* after the ASCII standard for text encoding.

Apple has always done a wonderful job of hiding the guts of WEP by allowing Mac users to enter a passphrase, such as "baby buggies," which the AirPort software converts into the appropriate hexadecimal number.

The main difficulty with using WEP, which is found in all Wi-Fi equipment, is that Mac users sometimes have problems in interchanging Apple's friendly text WEP passwords and the more generally accepted hexadecimal and ASCII keys. And entering 26 hexadecimal digits is no one's idea of a good time.

WEP's weakness

Starting in 2001, unfortunately, several flaws began to emerge that made it possible to extract the WEP key by examining sufficient traffic passing over the network. A few pieces of free software now automate this process for crackers with no knowledge of WEP.

WEP is therefore no longer reliable for businesses that move substantial amounts of traffic over their wireless networks: as little as 15 minutes of Wi-Fi sniffing can enable software to break the key on a fully loaded network. But even busy home networks might require a day to a week of solid observation to break, which means that most home users have nothing to worry about.

If someone is determined to break into a low-traffic network, that person might be able to flood your network with packets that cause your base station to generate traffic, thus producing the volume needed to crack the WEP key. This flooding technique isn't built into any of the free software that I'm aware of, but that could change at any time.

If you're really concerned, you can upgrade your software or your gear to support *WPA* (Wi-Fi Protected Access), which is widely available in all newer Wi-Fi equipment, and described in *Protect More Easily with WPA*. WPA doesn't suffer from any of these flaws.

NOTE   The new setup assistant that comes with AirPort Express lets you bypass some of the more obscure settings for WEP and WPA by reducing the number of options you need to sort through.

Setting up WEP on an all-AirPort network

You can set up WEP on all AirPort base stations.

First, enter a key on the base station:

1. Run AirPort Admin Utility and connect to your base station.

2. Turn on 128-bit WEP:

   In AirPort Admin Utility 3.4: Click Show All Settings, click the AirPort tab, and then click Change Wireless Security. From the pop-up menu, choose 128-bit WEP.

   In AirPort Admin Utility 4.0: In the AirPort tab, click the Security Options button. Then, from the Wireless Security pop-up menu, choose 128-bit WEP.

TIP   You could choose 40-bit, but 128-bit does provide additional (though not exponential) security. However, if you are using AirPort and non-AirPort equipment together, using a 128-bit key requires entry of 26 hexadecimal digits on non-AirPort devices.

3. Enter your password phrase in Network Password and Verify Password, and then click OK.

4. Click Update to have the base station recognize the new encryption settings.

Next, enter the key on your AirPort or AirPort Extreme-equipped client Macs:

- **In Mac OS 9:**

  1. Choose your network from the AirPort menu in the Control Strip (or run the AirPort application), expand the window by clicking the expansion triangle, and choose your network from the Choose Network pop-up menu.

  2. In the dialog box that appears, enter your AirPort password.

- **In Mac OS X:**

  1. Choose the network from the AirPort menu on the menu bar (or run Internet Connect in the Applications folder and choose the network from the AirPort tab's Network pop-up menu).

  2. In the dialog that appears, choose WEP Password from the Wireless Security pop-up menu (**Figure 34**), and enter it twice in the fields provided.

Figure 34

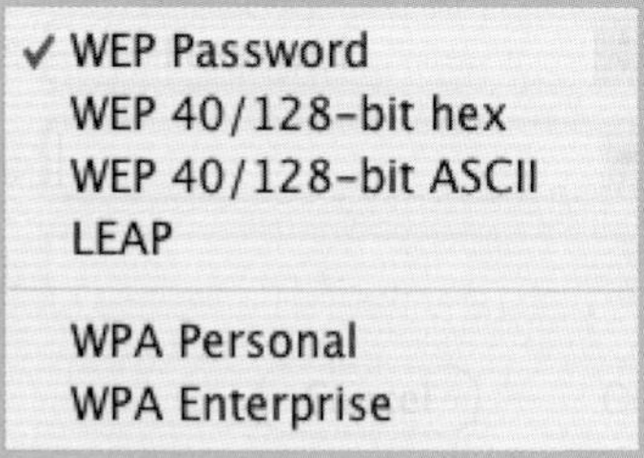

✓ WEP Password
WEP 40/128-bit hex
WEP 40/128-bit ASCII
LEAP

WPA Personal
WPA Enterprise

Apple's WEP password is the first choice. The other choices are explained ahead, in *Join a WEP-protected, non-AirPort network with any AirPort card.*

Extracting an AirPort key for a non-AirPort adapter

Any computer that wants to join a WEP-protected AirPort network and doesn't have an AirPort or AirPort Extreme Card in it—whether it's a Mac or a Windows or a Linux box—needs the hexadecimal equivalent of the Apple WEP password. Fortunately, it's easy to obtain:

1. Run AirPort Admin Utility and connect to your base station.

2. Choose Base Station > Equivalent Network Password.

TIP   You may want to make a screen capture of this hexadecimal key or type it into a text document to have it handy, especially if the key is a 128-bit WEP password— 26 characters long! Press Command-Shift-4 to select an area of the screen in Mac OS X to capture. Mac OS X records the selected area as a PDF file saved on the Desktop.

Connecting to an AirPort network from Windows XP

With a WEP key in hand, you can easily connect to any AirPort base station from Windows XP. Even if you don't normally run Windows XP, you may need this information in order to help visiting friends or relatives connect to your network.

1. In the System Tray, right-click your wireless connection and choose View Available Wireless Networks. (Or, click the Start button, choose My Network Places, click View Network Connections from Network Tasks at upper left, right-click your wireless connection, and choose View Available Wireless Networks.)

2. Click Advanced (Windows XP or XP Service Pack 1) or Change Advanced Settings (Windows XP Service Pack 2).

3. Select your network from the Preferred Networks list at the bottom of the Wireless Network Connection Properties dialog. (In Service Pack 2, first click the Wireless Networks tab.)

4. Click Properties.

5. From the Network Authentication pop-up menu, choose Shared. Then, from the Data Encryption pop-up menu, choose WEP (**Figure 35**).

Figure 35

Before you enter your key, choose Shared from Network Authentication and WEP from Data Encryption. Also, uncheck The Key Is Provided for Me Automatically.

If your dialog doesn't look like this one, use Windows Update or your computer maker's Web site to install the latest Windows wireless patches. Then, try these steps again.

6. Uncheck The Key Is Provided for Me Automatically.

7. Enter your WEP key twice without a dollar sign or any other preceding characters. Just enter it straight; for example, you might type E9234AB899 for a 40-bit WEP key. You enter it first in the Network Key field and then again in the Confirm Network Key field. Since you can't see the key as you type it, you can't verify visually that you have typed it correctly. Retyping the key helps ensure that you've entered it correctly.

8. Click OK, and then OK again.

9. If these steps fail to connect you to your network, follow Step 1 to bring up the View Available Wireless Networks connection again, choose your network, and then click Connect.

Join a WEP-protected, non-AirPort network with any AirPort card

If you adopt a wireless gateway other than Apple's, you might run into some confusion when trying to enter a WEP key on a Mac with an AirPort or AirPort Extreme Card.

First, set your key in the wireless gateway in either hexadecimal or ASCII as either 40/64 or 104/128 bits. If you're joining a network set up by other people, obtain the key from them.

Second, connect your Mac to the gateway. In versions of the Mac OS before 10.2, including 8.6 and 9.x, you can enter WEP keys only in one of two ways in any dialog that prompts for the key when joining the network:

•   **For a hexadecimal WEP key:** Enter $ (dollar sign) first, and then follow it with the hex key with no spaces, like $FEEB998877.

•   **For an ASCII WEP key:** Surround the key with double quotation marks, like "frech". Those are straight quotes, not curly quotes.

Starting with Mac OS X 10.2, however, you can choose the kind of WEP key from a pop-up menu (**Figure 34**, a few pages ago). Although you can still use a dollar sign or quotation marks, you can also just choose either WEP 40/128-bit Hex or WEP 40/128-bit ASCII from the pop-up menu and ignore the extra characters necessary in previous versions of the Mac OS.

NOTE   There's a way to use WEP more securely in which you must log into the network. If you're on a network like that, see *Log In Securely with WEP or WPA-Enterprise*.

PROTECT MORE EASILY WITH WPA

When I said earlier that WEP had major security weaknesses that weren't entirely applicable to home and small-business users, I also noted that there was a solution: WPA (Wi-Fi Protected Access). WPA was developed by The Wi-Fi Alliance to bridge the gap between WEP and a standard known as 802.11i. An engineering group ratified 802.11i in June 2004, but firmware and software updates to allow its additional features probably won't appear until later in 2004 at the earliest. None of its new features are a reason to wait on using Wi-Fi or deploying WPA security.

WPA fixes the methods by which security can be compromised, and makes the overall system less likely to be broken. WPA is available as a firmware upgrade for almost all older adapters, and either as an upgrade or as part of the shipping product for all newer hardware released since late 2002. Since the end of 2003, WPA must be built in to any new device that uses the Wi-Fi certification mark.

WPA's big advantage is that although it can use a hexadecimal key— one that's 64 hex digits long!—all platforms, not just the Macintosh, allow you to enter a more easily remembered text passphrase with punctuation, like `Rufus ate_my!water ba11oon.`

TIP	Researchers believe that WPA keys are susceptible to cracking through brute force if you choose keys that are shorter than 20 characters long and contain only dictionary words. Choosing short random numbers, letters, and punctuation, or longer passphrases with a few punctuation marks defeats this problem, as in the example passphrase above.

The original AirPort Base Station cannot be upgraded to WPA, but the AirPort Extreme and AirPort Express Base Stations support it. All AirPort and AirPort Extreme Cards can use WPA, but only within Mac OS X 10.3: older systems lack WPA support.

TIP	If you want to upgrade an older non-AirPort adapter for WPA, check out this article I wrote that links to the various firmware upgrades for cards as old as those made in 1999: http://wifinetnews.com/archives/002875.html.

Although it's technically possible for a base station to support WPA and WEP simultaneously, only SMC offers units with this capability—which reduces the network's security down to WEP's weaker level! More typically, you must set either WPA or WEP as the encryption mode and make sure that if you choose WPA that all your computers have the right updates to handle it as well.

Turning on WPA with AirPort Extreme

To turn on WPA, follow these steps:

1. Run AirPort Admin Utility 3.4 and connect to your base station.
2. Click Name & Password or click Show All Settings.
3. Click Change Wireless Security and choose WPA Personal from the pop-up menu.

NOTE WPA Personal uses a fixed key entered manually in the base station and all connected adapters. WPA Enterprise requires a special authentication server that allows you to log in with a user name and password but not a key; the server creates a master key for each computer's session, and then creates special keys from that master that are assigned to the gateway and each connected computer. These keys can be automatically changed quite frequently during a connection session without user involvement. See *Log In Securely with WEP or WPA-Enterprise*.

With a Personal key, each user on the network can still potentially see all the traffic of other users; with Enterprise, that's impossible.

4. If you leave the pop-up menu that appears set to Password, enter a key of 8 to 63 characters, including most punctuation. If you change the pop-up to Pre-Shared Key, you must enter 64 hexadecimal digits.
5. Click Update and wait for the base station to reboot.

You can now use the same password to connect from any WPA-capable system.

Connecting with AirPort or AirPort Extreme under Mac OS X 10.3 to a WPA network

Follow these steps to make a connection:

1. Choose the network you want to connect to from the AirPort menu.
2. At the password prompt, choose WPA Personal from the pop-up menu.
3. Enter the password or hexadecimal key, and click OK.

Connecting from Windows XP to a WPA network

To make the connection, follow these steps:

1. In the System Tray, right-click your wireless connection and choose View Available Wireless Networks. (Or, click the Start button, choose My Network Places, click View Network Connections from Network Tasks at upper left, right-click your wireless connection, and choose View Available Wireless Networks.)

2. Click Advanced (Windows XP or XP Service Pack 1) or Change Advanced Settings (Windows XP Service Pack 2).

3. Select your network from the Preferred Networks list at the bottom of the Wireless Network Connection Properties dialog. (In Service Pack 2, first click the Wireless Networks tab.)

4. Click Properties.

5. Set network authentication to WPA-PSK, and set data encryption to TKIP (**Figure 36**).

Figure 36

Choose WPA-PSK and TKIP in order to enter your WPA key.

If your dialog doesn't look like the one shown here, use Windows Update or your computer maker's Web site to install the latest Windows wireless patches. Then, try these steps again.

6. Uncheck The Key is Provided for Me Automatically.

7. Enter your key twice without a dollar sign or any other preceding

characters. Just enter it straight; for example, you might type E9234AB899 for a 40-bit key. You enter it first in the Network Key field and then again in the Confirm Network Key field. Since you can't see the key as you type it, you can't verify visually that you have typed it correctly. Retyping the key helps ensure that you've entered it correctly.

8. Click OK, and then OK again.

9. If these steps fail to connect you to your network, follow Step 1 to bring up the View Available Wireless Networks connection again, choose your network, and then click Connect.

LOG IN SECURELY WITH WEP OR WPA-ENTERPRISE

Small businesses are increasingly making use of an obscurely named technology that lets you log in with a user name and a password to a wireless network. This technology allows anyone to associate to an access point, but the access point restricts access to the wired network that it's connected to, including the Internet, until a user is successfully authenticated. Even better, each session you start with your user name causes a unique key to be generated for your session: even other users on the same network can't crack your traffic.

The latest in a long series of technical names

This system is called—take a deep breath—*IEEE 802.1X with EAP*. As noted early in this book, IEEE is an engineering group that sets standards. The 802.1 working group handles overall network standards. The "X" (capitalized) is the letter for that standard; don't confuse 802.1X (a standard) with 802.11x (a poor way to refer to the entire 802.11 family of wireless standards).

EAP stands for Encapsulated Authentication Protocol. It's a generic way to send authentication messages—messages about logging in—between the parts of a system that handle accounts and access. It's much like the PPP (Point-to-Point Protocol) that's used for dial-up access. In 802.1X, your machine can associate with an access point, but not send data until the access point has confirmed that you're a legitimate user. An 802.1X-enabled access point uses EAP to exchange credentials with an authentication server (which knows your user account information).

Once you successfully prove yourself to the authentication server, the server tells the access point to give you access. The server also creates a WEP or WPA encryption key and can continue to change this key regularly and automatically. No human hands are involved in typing keys, and each user has a unique key during his session. (In the case of WPA, the server creates a master key from which the actual WPA encryption key is derived, but it's effectively the same process from your viewpoint.)

Difficulties in enabling 802.1X with EAP

To use 802.1X with EAP on your network, you must solve two problems: first, it sends the credentials in the clear; second, it's expensive and difficult to operate an authentication server. You can solve the first problem with "tunneled EAP," in which a secure, SSL-like session packages your login information to prevent its interception.

NOTE Potential *man-in-the-middle attacks* for even tunneled 802.1X with EAP could allow a cracker to pose as an access point through which you log in. If your credentials were stolen in such a scenario, they could be "replayed" or sent again by the cracker to gain network access.

Avoid man-in-the-middle attacks by always paying careful attention to the digital certificate that's part of the secured EAP transaction. See Step 7 in *Connect via 802.1X /EAP with Mac OS X 10.3*.

The second problem is trickier. If you'd like to use 802.1X with EAP, you might have to figure out how to configure and run an expensive server or install the open-source FreeRADIUS software, which can be a chore.

I have found one reasonable, inexpensive option if you need this kind of security in a small office: the Gateway 7000 series of wireless access points. Gateway is best known for selling computers in cow-branded boxes, but the company also makes other gear. The 7000 series (an 802.11g and an 802.11a/g unit) has a built-in authentication server that works fine with Macs. The 802.11g version costs $299; the 802.11a/g version is $399. You can set up a couple of dozen user accounts with it. The Gateway devices are access points, not gateways; ironically, they don't offer Internet-connection sharing or other gateway features.

Connect via 802.1X/EAP with Mac OS X 10.3

Apple fully supports 802.1X/EAP through Internet Connect. Let me show you how easy it is to use with a Gateway 802.11g access point.

1. Run Internet Connect (find it in the Applications folder).

2. Choose File > New 802.1X Connection.

3. From the Configuration menu, choose Edit Configurations.

4. Click the + (plus) button at the lower left and enter your user account details (**Figure 37**).

Figure 37

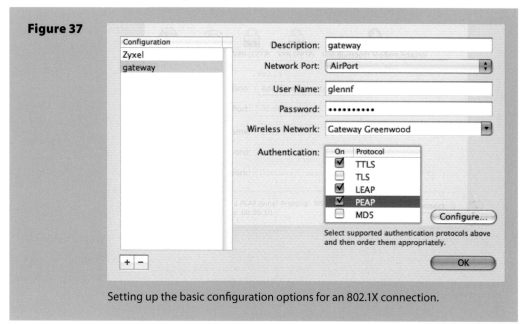

Setting up the basic configuration options for an 802.1X connection.

5. Choose your network from the Wireless Network pop-up menu. Under Authentication, uncheck options that won't be used. LEAP, TTLS, and PEAP are the only three secure methods of EAP. TLS requires installing a special digital certificate, and MD5 is entirely insecure for authentication. Click OK when you finish.

6. In the main 802.1X connection screen, click Connect to start a session (**Figure 38**).

Figure 38

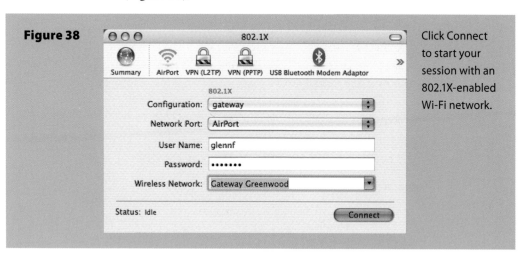

Click Connect to start your session with an 802.1X-enabled Wi-Fi network.

7. The access point wants to start a secure session with you. To do so, it first must provide you with its digital certificate, which is the basis of SSL-style security. The access point sends the certificate to Internet Connect, which presents you with details about it, and asks you to confirm it (**Figure 39**). Click Accept All to proceed.

Figure 39

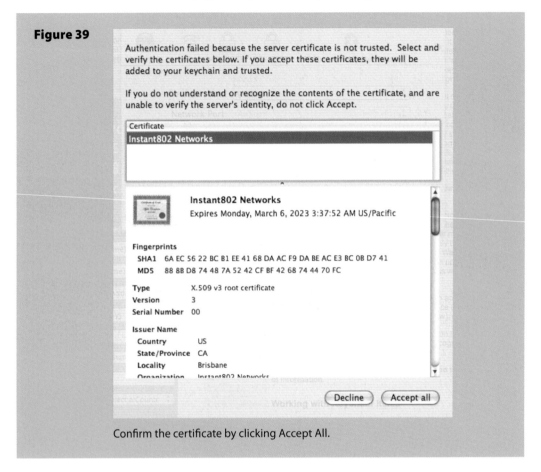

Authentication failed because the server certificate is not trusted. Select and verify the certificates below. If you accept these certificates, they will be added to your keychain and trusted.

If you do not understand or recognize the contents of the certificate, and are unable to verify the server's identity, do not click Accept.

Certificate
Instant802 Networks

Instant802 Networks
Expires Monday, March 6, 2023 3:37:52 AM US/Pacific

Fingerprints
SHA1   6A EC 56 22 BC B1 EE 41 68 DA AC F9 DA BE AC E3 BC 0B D7 41
MD5   88 8B D8 74 48 7A 52 42 CF BF 42 68 74 44 70 FC

Type   X.509 v3 root certificate
Version   3
Serial Number 00

Issuer Name
  Country   US
  State/Province CA
  Locality   Brisbane
  Organization Instant802 Networks

Decline   Accept all

Confirm the certificate by clicking Accept All.

NOTE
When you connect to a Web server that uses SSL, the server sends you certificate information. But because you already have a connection to the Internet, your browser automatically checks the validity of the Web server's certificate by consulting a built-in list of certificate authorities that vouch for most secure Web certificates.

Since 802.1X is predicated on not yet being connected to the Internet, you must accept the access point's certificate on its own merit before creating the secure session unless the access point's certificate has been signed by those built-in certificate authorities. Some access points, like the Gateway, use a self-signed certificate that no other authority vouches for.

These self-signed certificates are stored on your system, and they are accessible through Keychain Access, which is located in /Applications/Utilities.

Finally, you're connected. The Gateway system uses Protected EAP (PEAP), and that name is noted in the Status line of the 802.1X connection dialog (**Figure 40**).

Figure 40

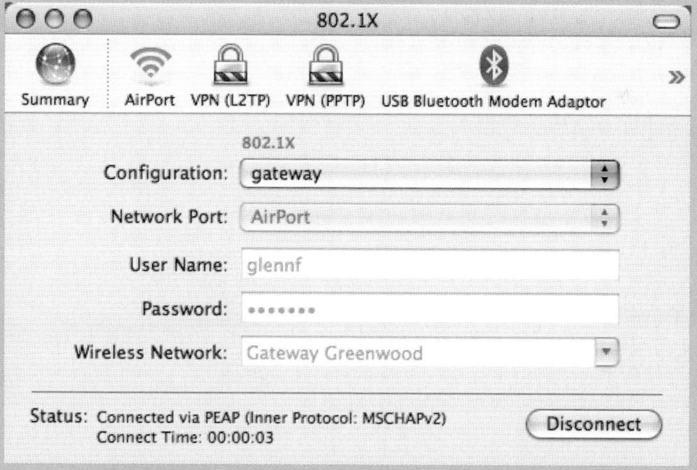

When you're connected to a server using 802.1X, you can see the duration of the connection and the method by which the connection was made (in this case, PEAP). Click Disconnect to end the session.

The next time you connect, you won't be prompted for a certificate because it's stored in your keychain. The only time you would ever see another prompt for that access point would be if someone were attempting to spoof it and convince you to connect to a masquerading, rogue access point. It won't happen in your home, but it happens in businesses regularly. As

802.1X starts to find its way into public hotspots—T-Mobile will be trying it in 2004—this masquerade might have serious consequences.

If you ever find yourself concerned about the certificate for the system you've connected to, you can review or delete the certificate by running Keychain Access (**Figure 41**). Finding its name might be tricky: for Gateway, it's listed as Instant802 Networks, which is the company that developed Gateway's firmware.

Figure 41

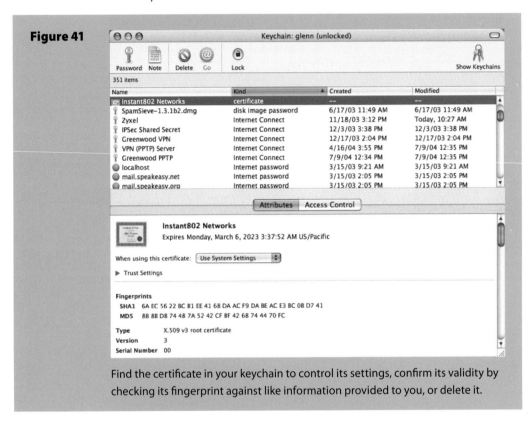

Find the certificate in your keychain to control its settings, confirm its validity by checking its fingerprint against like information provided to you, or delete it.

DEPLOY APPLICATION SECURITY

When discussing security previously, I've primarily covered methods of securing your network against someone joining it, and secondarily discussed how to prevent your traffic from being decoded and observed. At times, though, you might want to allow anyone to join a network, but still protect your own traffic over the network. This allows the best of both worlds: you can offer an open access point while keeping your data private.

The tips in this section are equally as useful for protecting data across a local network as they are for using a public hotspot network, which, by its nature, tends to lack any data encryption.

Each of these techniques encrypts data—from a single password up to all traffic entering and leaving your computer. Depending on what level of security you want, these tips should provide you with peace of mind and freedom from interception.

Secure Webmail

Reading email via a Web browser is an increasingly common task, especially with Webmail services that can connect behind the scenes to a "real" email server running the common POP or IMAP standards. But anything you read via a Web browser is sent in plain text.

To protect Webmail sessions, choose a provider that offers *SSL* (Secure Sockets Layer) connections. An SSL connection encrypts all traffic, rendering it impenetrable to anyone else.

Fastmail.fm (http://fastmail.fm/) and Google's Gmail service (currently in beta at http://gmail.google.com/) offer secure Webmail. Fastmail.fm requires a $14.95 one-time payment for SSL-based access, while Gmail includes it (currently) for free.

TIP Gmail isn't advertising its SSL feature in beta, but it's easy to reach. Enter https://gmail.google.com/ to log into your Gmail account instead of http://gmail.google.com/.

FTP over SSH

If you're exchanging files via FTP with remote servers, you might try a newer form of secure FTP that uses *SSH* (Secure Shell) to encrypt the connection. To use FTP with SSH, the remote server must have an SSH software server running.

SSH is a built-in part of Mac OS X, and can be enabled through System Preferences alongside FTP:

1. Open the Sharing preference pane in System Preferences.

2. In the Services tab, check the Remote Login box to enable SSH and check the FTP Access box to enable FTP.

On the client side, use FTP software that can handle the SSH connection, such as Interarchy from Stairways Software (http://www.stairways.com/). In Interarchy, select options from the File menu's SFTP submenu to connect to an FTP server over SSH.

SSL email

Some ISPs offer SSL email in which your email client initiates an SSL connection for sending and receiving mail. All current versions of popular email clients for Mac OS X, including Entourage, Mailsmith, Apple Mail, and Eudora, support SSL email. Check with your ISP to see if that's an option; you may have to do no more than check a few boxes in your account setup to turn SSL email on for either or both POP/IMAP and SMTP.

APOP and Authenticated SMTP

If you're concerned only with protecting your email passwords (which may be the same as passwords used for other services) and not about the contents of your email, you can encrypt your email passwords by using *APOP* (Authenticated POP) and *Authenticated SMTP*.

Both require that your ISP offer the service at the server level, and both are simple to set up in any mail client. With APOP, you enter your password in your email program, but the program sends a unique one-time password to the server—it's essentially a disposable password that you don't have to manage.

Authenticated SMTP allows you to send email from any network, and it typically uses an encrypted login that protects your email password in the process. It can also use a fully encrypted SSL session, which is increasingly typical and, in fact, recommended by a recent anti-spam report issued by major ISPs.

VPN

The whole 9 yards of data-in-transit protection is a *VPN* (virtual private network). A VPN protects all the data entering and leaving your computer by encrypting it on its departure and decrypting it on its arrival.

A VPN requires that you connect to a VPN server that manages the secure tunnel formed between your computer and itself. Mac OS X Server 10.3 includes both major flavors of VPN servers: *PPTP* (Point-to-Point Tunneling Protocol) and *IPsec-over-L2TP* (IPsec protocol over Layer 2 Tunneling Protocol).

TIP   Mac OS X Server 10.3 is just $499 for 10 simultaneous users—and VPN users aren't counted against the total maximum simultaneous logins. This 10-user license can be an inexpensive solution for a small business to maintain local and remote network security.

Mac OS X 10.2 included an easy-to-use PPTP client, whereas 10.3 has both PPTP and IPsec. Both clients are built into the Internet Connect program found in the Applications folder.

To use a VPN, you first set up accounts on a server, and then turn on the VPN service in either or both flavors. Then you run a VPN client, provide the VPN server's address, enter a user name and password (for PPTP and IPsec) and an additional "shared secret" (for IPsec), and connect.

Once you've connected, all your traffic is encrypted until you disconnect. I've found that I can set up a VPN connection even over the slowest cellular data connection—9600 bits per second!

VPNs aren't for everyone, but they are an efficient way to protect your data when you have the right pieces in place.

Appendix A: Setting up AirPort Express

In this appendix, I walk you through installing and configuring an AirPort Express, explain how to reset an AirPort Express, and show you how to use AirPort Express from iTunes to play music through your stereo.

Not surprisingly, given Apple's penchant for making routine tasks simpler whenever possible, the company has provided two separate ways to configure AirPort Express:

- AirPort Express Assistant, a setup wizard that walks you through steps and choices
- AirPort Admin Utility, the same tool used to configure AirPort and AirPort Extreme Base Stations

NOTE Any experience you might already have with configuring an AirPort Extreme Base Station will translate easily to AirPort Express, especially if you aren't setting up music streaming.

INSTALL AIRPORT EXPRESS

Here are step-by-step directions for installing your AirPort Express:

1. Plug your AirPort Express into a power outlet that's adjacent to whatever you want to use it with, like a stereo and/or USB printer.

2. Connect it to the network using one of these methods:

   Ethernet: plug in the Ethernet cable that leads to your switch or broadband modem.

   Wireless: you don't need to do anything so long as the device is within range of the main base station.

TIP If your AirPort Express won't fit when you try to plug it into an existing outlet or power strip—it connects directly to the outlet—you can purchase Apple's $39 add-on kit, which is ponderously called the "AirPort Express Stereo Connection Kit with Monster Cables." The kit includes a several-foot-long, snap-in power cord with a three-prong plug at the end.

3. Open the CD-ROM that came with the AirPort Express on any Mac running Mac OS X 10.3 that's connected to your Ethernet network or located near the AirPort Express you just plugged in. In the CD-ROM's

window, double-click Install AirPort and iTunes. (You can copy the manuals to your hard disk later, if you need them.)

4. Click Continue when the installer asks if it can run a program to determine if the software can be installed, and then click Continue again in the first screen.

5. Look over the Read Me information and click Continue.

6. Accept the license on the following screen by clicking Continue and then Agree.

7. Select the Destination volume for the software and click Continue.

8. If you have AirPort or iTunes software already installed (this is likely), click Custom Install. In **Figure 42**, you can see that because iTunes 4.6 was already installed the installer knew to just upgrade the AirPort software. (iTunes is checked but shows 0 bytes needed for the upgrade.)

    If you don't have AirPort or iTunes software installed, click Install.

Figure 42

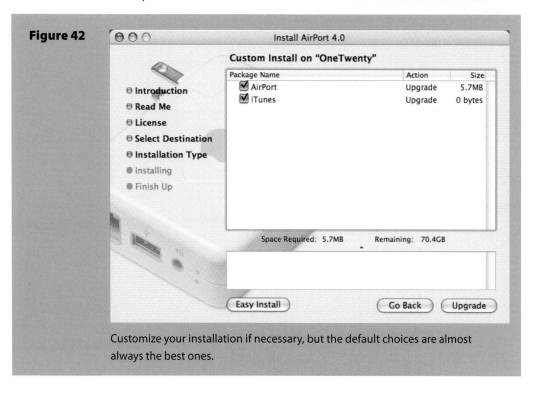

Customize your installation if necessary, but the default choices are almost always the best ones.

9. After the installation is finished, click Finish.

10. Before you restart to complete the process, review *Connect before Configuring*, (next) and follow any steps there that apply to your situation.

11. When you're ready, restart the Mac to complete the installation.

After restarting, the Macintosh automatically launches the AirPort Express Assistant.

NOTE When you install an AirPort Express, all copies of iTunes on the network can stream music to the base station via AirTunes. I talk more about that later in this appendix, in *Play Music with iTunes.*

CONNECT BEFORE CONFIGURING

Before you can configure, you must connect. Work your way through each item in this section to make certain you are connected correctly and that your access control list is updated.

Connect to the AirPort Express directly

To avoid complications with a wireless-only configuration where the base station is not connected to Ethernet, connect to the AirPort Express before starting the configuration, using its default network name. (Generally, if you connected the AirPort Express to a local Ethernet network before configuring, you can skip this step.)

To do so, choose the default network name from the AirPort menu in the menu bar. (Or, you can choose it in Internet Connect's AirPort tab.)

NOTE *What is the default network name?* The default network name is "AirPort Network 0033FF" where "0033FF" is replaced with the last six digits of the AirPort ID (MAC address) of the wireless adapter in the AirPort Express. That number is printed on the electrical-plug side of the AirPort Express.

Add the base station to your access control list

If you have an existing network with an access control list in place, you must update it to list your AirPort Express Base Station. Access control lists allow you to restrict which wireless devices can connect to a Wi-Fi gateway. If you try to configure your AirPort Express on an existing network with an access control list in place, you will find yourself mystified as to why the AirPort Express Assistant can't connect to your AirPort Express. (It shouldn't be an issue, but it appears that the assistant relies on the base station of your existing network for certain information.)

Here's how to update an access control list for any AirPort base station:

1. Run AirPort Admin Utility and connect to your base station.

2. Click the Access Control tab.

3. Click the + (plus) button and enter the AirPort ID (the AirPort ID is printed on the electrical-plug side of the AirPort Express).

4. Click OK.

5. Click Update to upload the new access control list and restart your base station.

Here's how to update an access control list for a Linksys WRT54G:

1. Connect to the administrative Web server of the WRT54G.

2. Click the Wireless tab, and then the Wireless MAC Filter tab.

3. Click the Edit MAC Filter button.

4. Add the AirPort ID of the AirPort Express (the AirPort ID is printed on the electrical-plug side of the AirPort Express).

5. In the main screen, click Save Settings to restart the gateway with its new settings.

CONFIGURE WITH THE AIRPORT EXPRESS ASSISTANT

AirPort Express Assistant is a new tool that hides much of the complexity of setting up and adding a base station, but it's designed entirely for AirPort Express: AirPort Extreme users are supposed to be, uh, more sophisticated. (If you need to locate it on your disk, you can find it in /Applications/Utilities/.)

Use the assistant for the first time

The assistant will run automatically after you restart following the installation process. Here's what to do:

1. **Introduction screen:** Click Continue to move to the next screen.

2. **Network Setup screen 1 (Figure 43):** Set the basic purpose of your base station by selecting the appropriate options.

Figure 43

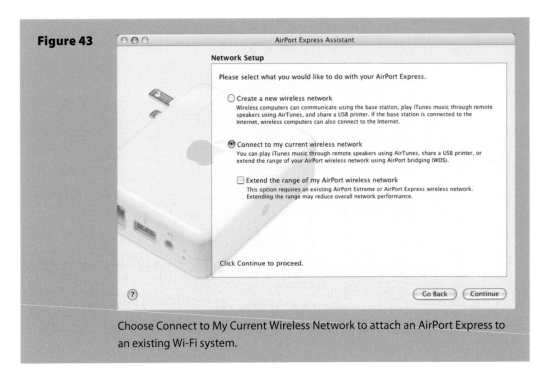

Choose Connect to My Current Wireless Network to attach an AirPort Express to an existing Wi-Fi system.

Create a new wireless network: Select this less common option to create a new wireless network to which clients can connect. If you choose it, the AirPort Express can share an Internet connection among Wi-Fi computers or connect via other gateway options (see *Take Control of Dynamically Assigned Addresses*). (I talk more about this choice later in *Configure with AirPort Admin Utility*, which you can refer to once you complete these steps.)

Connect to my current wireless network: When you select this more common option, a checkbox appears below it. If you leave the checkbox unchecked, the AirPort Express functions only as a client, and cannot accept wireless connections from Wi-Fi adapters. It can connect to any wireless network and stream music and share a USB printer. Check the box if you have an AirPort Extreme or AirPortExpress Base Station already installed, and wish to turn on WDS. By turning on WDS, you make it possible to connect your AirPort Express Base Station wirelessly to your AirPort Extreme or AirPortExpress Base Station. (See *Bridge Wirelessly* to learn how to set up an existing base station to support WDS; or you can let the assistant automatically set it up for you.)

3. **Network Setup screen 2 (Figure 44):** The next screen displays any AirPort Express networks that the assistant finds. (See *Connect before Configuring*, earlier, if you don't see any networks.) The network name

will be "AirPort Network" plus the last six digits of the AirPort ID for the base station you're adding.

Figure 44

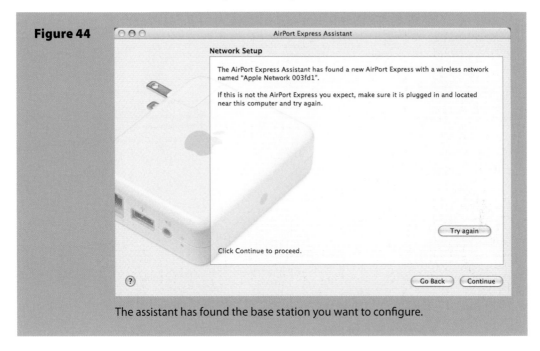

The assistant has found the base station you want to configure.

If you're configuring multiple AirPort Express units at once: Note which base station has which AirPort ID.

If you're connecting as a client to a wireless network: Choose that network from the Wireless Network Name pop-up menu. Enter the network password if one exists.

4. **Network Setup screen 3 (Figure 45):** Secure your AirPort Express by entering the same password twice. If you check Remember This Password, the assistant can connect to the base station automatically the next time you run the software. In the AirPort Express Name field, enter the name you would like to appear in iTunes under the list of remote speakers. This is also the name used to identify the base station in AirPort Admin Utility or if you use the assistant again. You can change the name later.

NOTE   If the network uses WPA, or if your WEP password or key doesn't work here, you need to abandon the AirPort Express Assistant and use AirPort Admin Utility, which offers more options for joining a secured network.

Figure 45

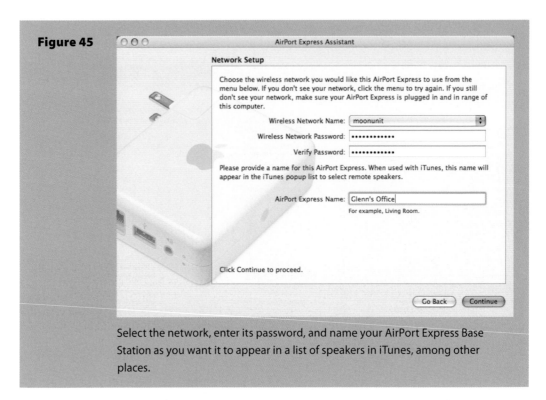

Select the network, enter its password, and name your AirPort Express Base Station as you want it to appear in a list of speakers in iTunes, among other places.

If you're connecting via WDS, an additional screen will prompt you to select the main base station for your network (**Figure 46**). Use the name and/or AirPort ID to pick the right one and click OK. You'll be prompted for the main base station's administrative password, and the assistant automatically configures your main base station after you successfully enter that password.

WARNING! When you use WDS to connect your AirPort Express to an existing wireless network, you can use only WEP encryption to protect the network. Apple's version of WDS has a limitation in how it rewrites packets that is incompatible with WPA. To use WPA, you must either use the AirPort Express in client-only mode, in which it can't serve as an extension of your network, or connect it to the network via Ethernet.

Figure 46

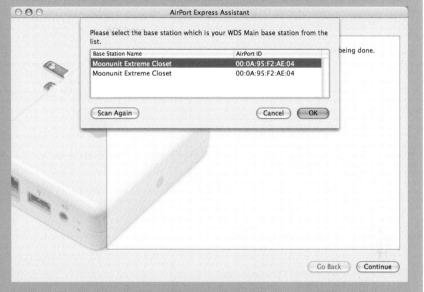

Select the main base station to which you are connecting your AirPort Express via WDS. In this figure, one base station is listed twice for unknown reasons.

SEVERE WARNING!

AirPort Extreme cannot connect via WDS to any AirPort Extreme or AirPort Express set up as a main base station unless that main base station has DHCP turned on to distribute addresses. Otherwise, the AirPort Express Assistant won't let you join (**Figure 47**). AirPort Admin Utility allows you to configure that connection, but then the AirPort Express requires a hard reset. However, you can avoid resetting the AirPort Express (via AirPort Admin Utility) by turning on Distribute IP Addresses on your main base station and rebooting it. This allows the AirPort Express to recover, but it might not be what you want for your network.

Figure 47

WDS Setup

The base station you selected as a WDS main base station is not distributing IP addresses. Please use AirPort Admin Utility to set up this base station to distribute IP addresses.

OK

AirPort Express Assistant warns you when you try to set up a WDS connection it can't support.

5. **Summary screen:** Click Show Passwords to confirm that the passwords you've entered are correct. Click Update to apply the settings.

6. **Final screen:** This screen confirms that the changes were made. Click Quit to exit the assistant.

Change settings with AirPort Express Assistant

You can run the assistant at any time to change basic setup items. (Use AirPort Admin Utility for advanced settings that aren't available in the assistant, like choosing whether to enable AirTunes over Ethernet.) In this example, I'm going to set up the AirPort Express Base Station as if there were no other wireless network, and the base station was plugged in to my broadband connection. Here are the steps:

1. **Introduction screen (Figure 48):** The assistant's Introduction screen prompts you with a different message on its subsequent runs. After the first few screens, though, the setup is exactly as if you were running it for the first time. Select Change Settings on an Existing AirPort Express.

Figure 48

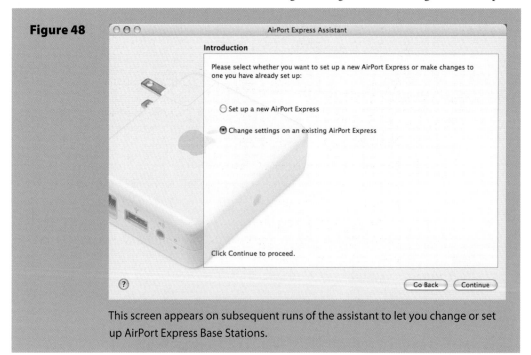

This screen appears on subsequent runs of the assistant to let you change or set up AirPort Express Base Stations.

2. **Network Setup screen 1:** Click Continue to reconfigure the base station in the Network Setup portion of the assistant.

3. **Network Setup screen 2 (Figure 49):** This screen displays your current settings, which you can change (notice that this screen has a pop-up

menu that offers a more extensive set of choices for your wireless security method). Although you can make changes here and click Continue, *to stay with these steps you should click Start Again* (at the lower left) to entirely reconfigure the unit.

Figure 49

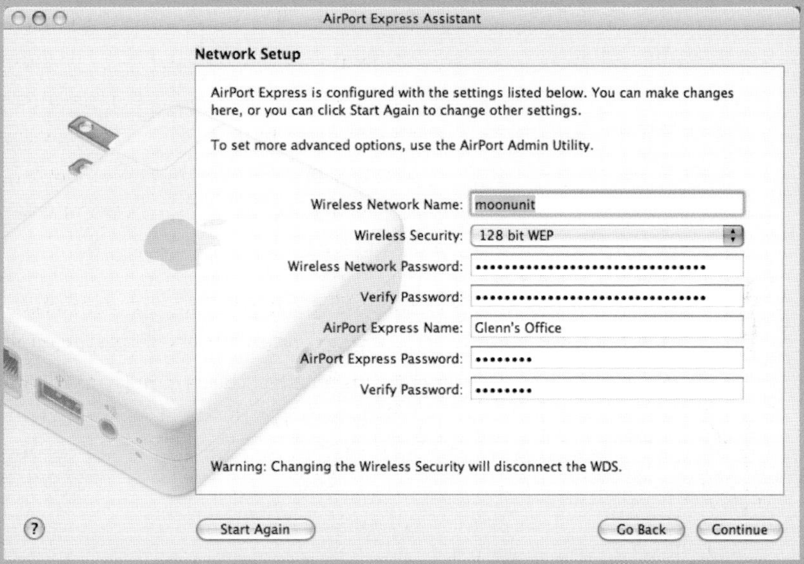

Make changes to basic settings in this screen or click Start Again to reconfigure from the beginning.

4. **Network Setup screen 3:** Select Create a New Wireless Network.

5. **Network Setup screen 4 (Figure 50):** You can now name your network and your AirPort Express separately. In **Figure 50**, I'm making a stand-alone network, so I entered a silly name. (To allow roaming among multiple Wi-Fi access points using Ethernet as the connector, enter the same network name in the Wireless Network Name field as you gave every other access point on the network.)

Figure 50

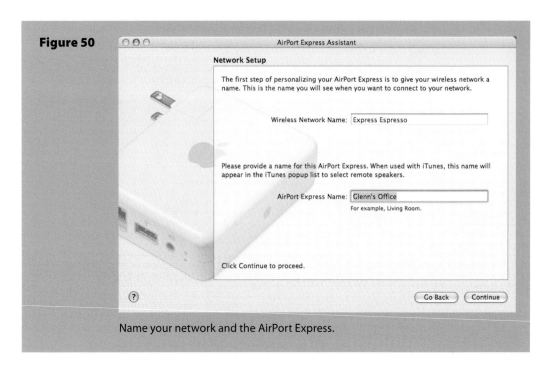

Name your network and the AirPort Express.

Figure 51

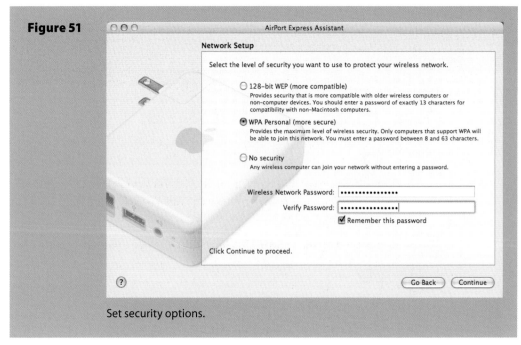

Set security options.

6. **Network Setup screen 5 (Figure 51):** Since all my computers are running Mac OS X 10.3 or Windows XP, I can select WPA Personal. For older computers, I recommend 128-bit WEP. Click Remember This Password to store your password in the keychain; that allows you to avoid re-entering this information if you use the assistant again. It also enables your computer to connect automatically to this network when you finish with the configuration.

7. **Internet Setup screen (Figure 52):** Select your Internet-connection method.

Figure 52

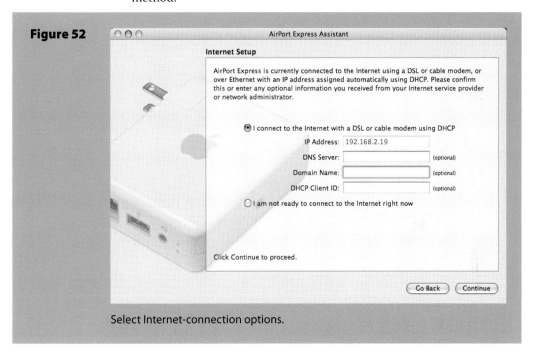

Select Internet-connection options.

If your ISP provides you with an IP address via DHCP: Leave the defaults as they stand: I Connect to the Internet with a DSL or Cable Modem Using DHCP.

If you need to set a static IP address, PPPoE, or other options: Select I Am Not Ready to Connect to the Internet Right Now, and after finishing this configuration, connect to the AirPort Express via AirPort Admin Utility to set those more advanced options.

8. **AirPort Express Setup screen:** Set or change the password for the AirPort Express. If you want the assistant or AirPort Admin Utility to bypass asking for it again, check Remember This Password.

9. **Summary screen (Figure 53):** This screen shows the options you've chosen, slightly abbreviated. If they're correct, click Update; otherwise,

click Go Back and change them. When you click Update, the AirPort Express reboots.

Figure 53

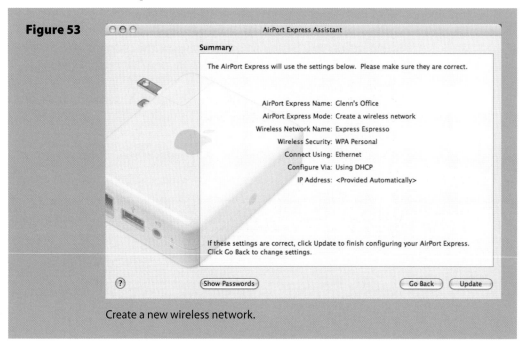

Create a new wireless network.

10. **Final screen:** After the gateway has successfully rebooted, the final screen appears. Click Quit to exit.

The assistant allows you to control what most users need to configure in an AirPort Express. But if you've read this far, you're probably part of a more network administrator-like group that needs the options found in AirPort Admin Utility, discussed next.

CONFIGURE WITH AIRPORT ADMIN UTILITY

AirPort Admin Utility is found in the Applications folder's Utilities folder. It can configure any Apple base station, including the original AirPort models, AirPort Extreme, and now AirPort Express. In this section, I explain how to advance to the Configuration display in AirPort Admin Utility and then give you an overview of what you can do on each of the configuration-related tabs.

NOTE AirPort Admin Utility 4.0 comes on the AirPort Express CD. This version of the utility removes a simplified tab from the left, and looks slightly different from the version you may be accustomed to using. I used version 4.0 in the figures for this appendix.

I doubt you'll have trouble getting to the Configuration display, but here are the steps.

1. Launch AirPort Admin Utility.

2. Select your AirPort Express and click Configure in the toolbar (or just double-click its entry in the list) (**Figure 54**). If your AirPort Express isn't listed, click the Other button and enter its IP address. Because AirPort gateways use OpenTalk (née Rendezvous) to identify themselves over local networks, there's usually a problem when you don't see the base station in the list.

Figure 54

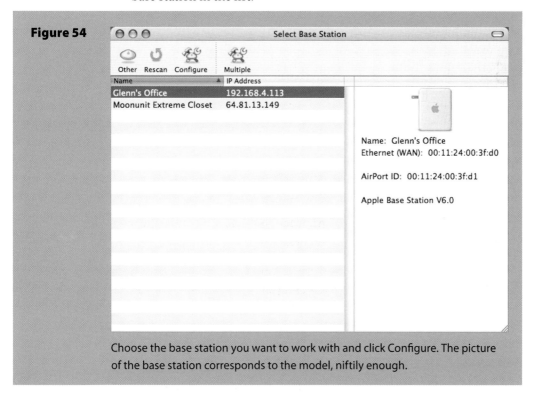

Choose the base station you want to work with and click Configure. The picture of the base station corresponds to the model, niftily enough.

TIP   You can also click Other to configure base stations with static IP addresses that are located outside of your local networks, even on the other side of the planet.

Now that you've reached the Configuration display, you'll see different options, depending on if your AirPort Express is in client mode or WDS mode:

• **Client mode:** Only three tabs appear in the Configuration display: AirPort, Internet, and Music.

- **WDS mode:** It looks just like an AirPort Extreme Base Station set to WDS, though it also includes the Express-specific options found in the AirPort tab and the additional Music tab. It lacks an Internet tab.

AirPort tab

The AirPort tab controls basic settings, as you can see in **Figure 55**. You can choose a mode from the Use Base Station To pop-up menu, and you'll see different settings depending on your choice. (For client mode, choose Join an Existing Wireless Network; for WDS mode, choose Create a Wireless Network.)

Figure 55

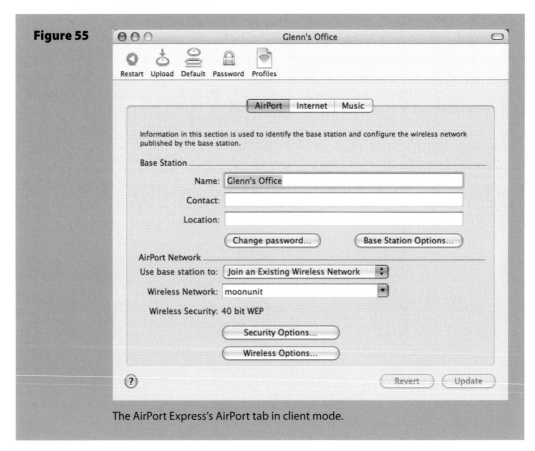

The AirPort Express's AirPort tab in client mode.

Base Station Options contains two features specific to AirPort Express. Click Base Station Options to bring up its dialog. The dialog has two particularly interesting settings, which I describe in **Figure 56**.

Figure 56

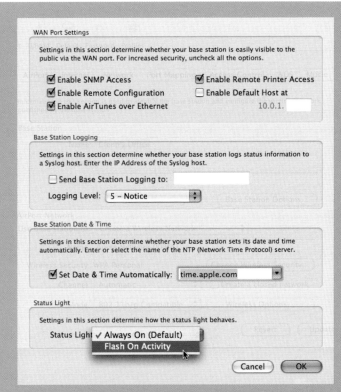

WAN Port Settings

Settings in this section determine whether your base station is easily visible to the public via the WAN port. For increased security, uncheck all the options.

☑ Enable SNMP Access   ☑ Enable Remote Printer Access
☑ Enable Remote Configuration   ☐ Enable Default Host at
☑ Enable AirTunes over Ethernet   10.0.1. [ ]

Base Station Logging

Settings in this section determine whether your base station logs status information to a Syslog host. Enter the IP Address of the Syslog host.

☐ Send Base Station Logging to: [   ]
Logging Level: [5 – Notice   ⬍]

Base Station Date & Time

Settings in this section determine whether your base station sets its date and time automatically. Enter or select the name of the NTP (Network Time Protocol) server.

☑ Set Date & Time Automatically: [time.apple.com ⬍]

Status Light

Settings in this section determine how the status light behaves.

Status Light [✓ Always On (Default)]
         [Flash On Activity]

(Cancel) (OK)

This dialog has two particularly interesting options:

- **Enable AirTunes over Ethernet:** Lets wired and wireless computers stream music. I can't think of why you might want to restrict this, but if you're concerned, leave the option on and password-protect the remote speakers (in the Music tab).

- **Status Light:** Always On makes the light green while the AirPort is in operation. (It flashes or is orange during reboot and startup.) Flash On Activity makes the light flicker to show network activity.

Internet tab

When your AirPort Express is in client mode, the Internet tab lets you enter a static IP address manually or pick up an IP address via DHCP (**Figure 57**).

Figure 57

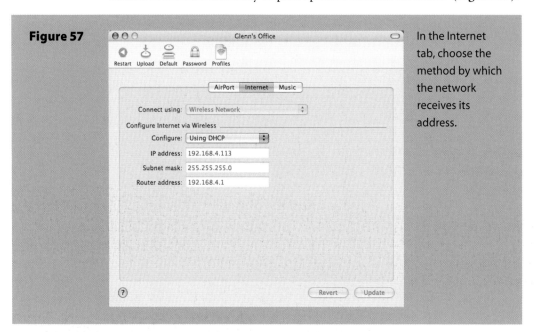

In the Internet tab, choose the method by which the network receives its address.

In WDS mode, the Connect Using menu is set to AirPort (WDS) and offers the same options as an AirPort Extreme Base Station in WDS mode: entering the main base station's MAC address, allowing or disallowing wireless clients, and setting an IP address or using DHCP to receive one automatically.

Music tab

The caption for **Figure 58** details what you need to know about using the Music tab to control music streaming and speaker settings.

Figure 58

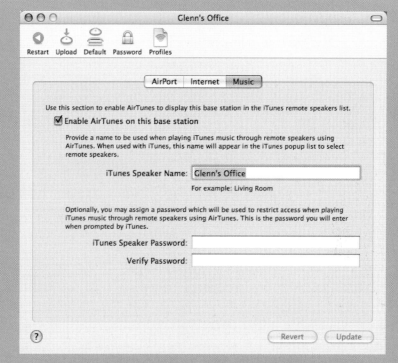

Set up streaming in the Music tab:

- **Enable AirTunes on This Base Station:** This box turns streaming on and off. (As noted earlier, streaming can be restricted to wireless computers.)

- **iTunes Speaker Name:** This name shows in the iTunes remote speaker list.

- **Password:** Set a password to limit use of this speaker set to people who have the password.

AirPort Express Profiles

AirPort Express supports a new feature for base stations, called Profiles. Profiles are a great way to pre-configure settings and not have to retrieve them tediously when you move an AirPort Express from place to place, or use the unit with different computers.

In *Working with a Model Configuration*, I describe how to save your configuration within AirPort Admin Utility as a file that you can load into a base station (whether the one you saved it from or another you want to configure identically). The new Profiles feature saves these configuration files in the AirPort Express Base Station itself, meaning that you can switch among them from any computer that has AirPort Admin Utility 4.0 installed.

To access profiles, click the Profiles button on the toolbar. A dialog appears that lets you create, rename, duplicate, delete, or switch profiles (**Figure 59**).

Figure 59

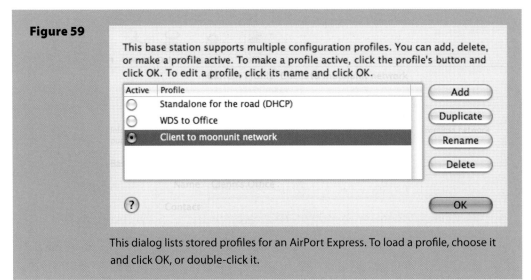

This dialog lists stored profiles for an AirPort Express. To load a profile, choose it and click OK, or double-click it.

When you choose a profile by selecting it and clicking OK, the profile loads into AirPort Admin Utility. To apply the profile to your base station, click Update. The base station will reboot.

RESET AIRPORT EXPRESS

If something goes wrong with your AirPort Express, a reset will often solve the problem. The Reset button is on the underside (jack side) of the unit, and you can use a paperclip to push it. There are three ways you can reset the AirPort Express, each of which has a different effect on your base station's stored settings and profiles.

TIP   Apple has a wonderfully clear document on the three reset modes of the AirPort Express base station, and I recommend reading it (http://docs.info.apple.com/article.html?artnum=108044).

Here's how to reset your AirPort Express:

• **Soft reset:** Resets the password while the AirPort Express is plugged in to the power outlet. Press the Reset button for one second to trigger a soft reset. Follow Apple's voluminous step-by-step instructions to reset the password.

• **Hard reset:** Resets the whole unit while it is plugged in to the power outlet, but keeps stored profiles (see *AirPort Express Profiles*). You can then reconnect to the device and restore a profile. Press in on the Reset button for 10 seconds to trigger a hard reset.

- **Factory reset:** Erases everything. Unplug the AirPort Express. Press the Reset button and plug the unit in to the power outlet. Keep on pressing in for a few seconds until you see the unit flash green four times. I recommend this option when you need to start from scratch.

PLAY MUSIC WITH ITUNES

iTunes 4.6 supports AirPort Express through the newly named AirTunes system for streaming music. It's simple to use, and my instructions assume that you have already configured your AirPort Express Base Station through the detailed advice earlier in this appendix.

Here are the steps for playing music via iTunes and AirPort Express:

1. In iTunes, choose File > Preferences, and click the Audio tab (**Figure 60**).

Figure 60

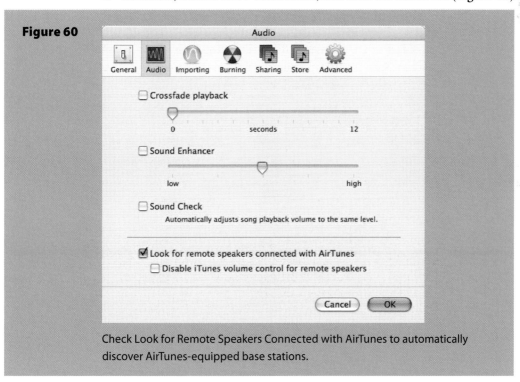

Check Look for Remote Speakers Connected with AirTunes to automatically discover AirTunes-equipped base stations.

2. Verify that the checkbox Look for Remote Speakers Connected with AirTunes is checked (look near the bottom of the tab). This option causes iTunes to be aware of AirPort Express Base Stations that are plugged into stereos or powered speakers.

3. If you want to control volume only from your stereo (and not also from iTunes), select Disable iTunes Volume Control for Remote Speakers.

4. Click OK.

   Now that you have a configured AirPort Express on the network and the Look for Remote Speakers Connected with AirTunes checkbox selected, iTunes should display a new pop-up menu with a speaker icon next to it in the lower right of its main display window (**Figure 61**).

Figure 61

Choose the AirPort Express to stream through from the pop-up menu at the lower right.

5. In iTunes, choose a base station from the new pop-up menu. The menu lists all the AirPort Express base stations connected to stereos; Computer means the audio output option you selected on your own computer in the Sound preference pane. You can choose only one item from the menu, so it isn't possible, for instance, to play music through your stereo and through your computer at once. You'll have to get your quadraphonic sound some other way.

   Congratulations—you've set up AirTunes!

Here are a few more things you might like to know about AirTunes:

- **Two people playing music at once:** If you try to play music through an AirPort Express that someone else is actively playing music through, iTunes notifies you when you press the Play button (**Figure 62**). If that person clicks Pause, iTunes releases that person's control of the speaker, and within 2–3 seconds, another user with iTunes can start playing music through that AirPort Express.

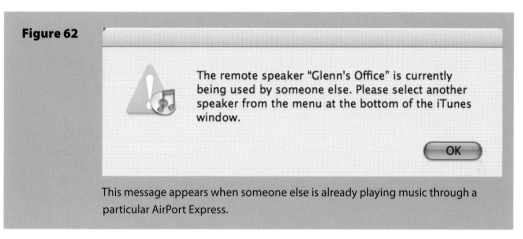

Figure 62

The remote speaker "Glenn's Office" is currently being used by someone else. Please select another speaker from the menu at the bottom of the iTunes window.

OK

This message appears when someone else is already playing music through a particular AirPort Express.

- **Password protection:** You can password-protect AirPort Express music streaming (as noted earlier). For instance, if you live in a dorm, you might want to prevent pranksters from blasting through your speakers. When you try to connect to protected base stations to play music, you must enter the password (**Figure 63**).

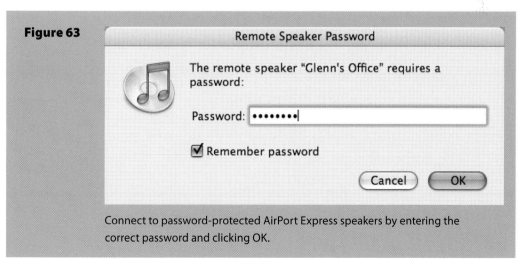

Figure 63

Remote Speaker Password

The remote speaker "Glenn's Office" requires a password:

Password: ••••••••

☑ Remember password

Cancel   OK

Connect to password-protected AirPort Express speakers by entering the correct password and clicking OK.

Password-protected speakers show in the list of speakers with a lock next to them (**Figure 64**).

Figure 64

The lock indicates that these speakers require a password.

Appendix B: Setting up a Software Base Station

You can use a computer equipped with a Wi-Fi adapter card not just as a client on a Wi-Fi network, but also as a base station. I discussed the pros and cons of this technique in *Consider a Software Base Station*. This section explains how to set up a software base station under Mac OS 8.6/9.x (next) and under Mac OS X (see *Configuring Internet Sharing in Mac OS X*).

TIP You can set up a software base station in Windows XP, too, through a combination of setting up an ad hoc network using one piece of configuration software, and the Internet-sharing feature that's similar to Mac OS X's.

SIDEBAR **SOFTWARE BASE STATION VS. AD HOC NETWORKS**

You don't need to create an ad hoc network (also known as a computer-to-computer network) before setting up a software base station, and in fact, the two are mutually exclusive. Use an ad hoc network for connecting with another computer when you have no Internet connection to share.

When you set up such a network by choosing Create Network from the AirPort menu, your Mac assigns itself an IP address in the 169.254.x.x range; Macs that connect to your network will pick up addresses in that range so they can communicate. OpenTalk (née Rendezvous) services like iChat should work fine over ad hoc networks; they're best used for transferring a file or chatting during a keynote speech.

CONFIGURING SOFTWARE BASE STATION IN MAC OS 8.6/9.X

To share an Internet connection among the wireless computers that connect to your Software Base Station, you must also have a working Internet connection via Ethernet from a cable or DSL modem, or via standard dialup.

You configure the Software Base Station feature in Mac OS 8.6 and 9.x via the AirPort application, typically found in the Apple Extras folder inside your Applications folder. Here are the steps:

1. Open the AirPort application and click the Software Base Station button in the main screen's lower-left corner to open the Software Base Station dialog box (**Figure 65**).

Figure 65

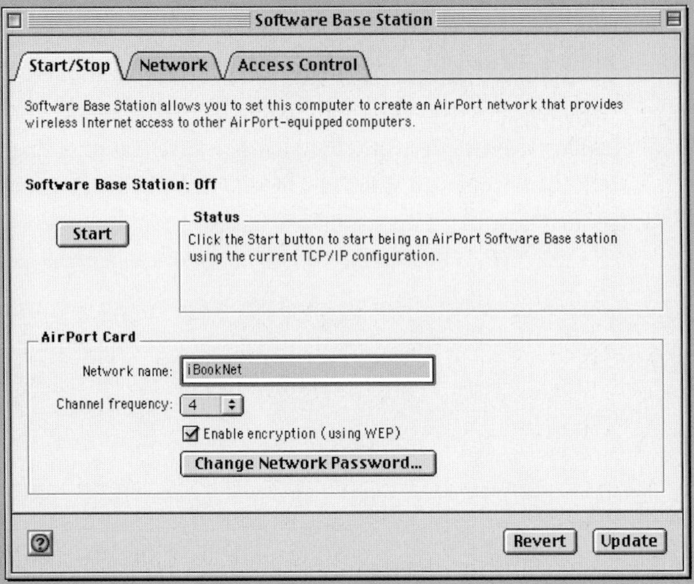

The Software Base Station dialog box in Mac OS 8.6/9.x.

2. In the Start/Stop tab, enter a name for your network—its service set identifier or SSID—in the Network Name field and choose the channel from the Channel Frequency pop-up menu.

3. If you want to protect your wireless data, check Enable Encryption (Using WEP) and click the Change Network Password button to enter the WEP key. Although Apple calls this WEP, you enter a plain text password that it converts into the actual WEP key.

WARNING! You can't use a non-AirPort wireless adapter to connect to an encrypted software base station because Apple didn't provide a tool in Mac OS 8.6/9.x's configuration that lets you extract the hexadecimal key necessary outside the AirPort environment. You can only enter an AirPort password and then use that password with other AirPort and AirPort Extreme Cards. See *Protect with WEP*.

4. Click Start to begin sharing the Internet connection.

Software Base Station always automatically provides private, non-routable IP addresses to client computers; in the Network tab, you can select if you also want to provide IP addresses to wired computers connected via Ethernet. Finally, use the Access Control tab to restrict access to specific network adapters by entering their MAC addresses, or the unique number assigned to the adapter.

> **TIP**
>
> If you're using a third-party wireless network adapter or want more control than Apple's Software Base Station feature provides in Mac OS 8.6/9.x, check out Sustainable Softworks' IPNetRouter (http://www.sustworks.com/site/prod_ipr_overview.html). It can do everything Software Base Station can do and much more, in part because Sustainable Softworks wrote much of Software Base Station for Apple.

CONFIGURING INTERNET SHARING IN MAC OS X

In Mac OS X 10.2 Jaguar and 10.3 Panther, Apple relocated the Software Base Station feature from the AirPort utility to the Sharing preference pane in System Preferences.

Before starting, make sure you have either an Ethernet or an Internal Modem connection set up in the Network preference pane, as you can't create a software access point without one or the other active. For this example, I assume your Internet connection comes via Ethernet from a cable modem.

1. In System Preferences, open the Sharing pane and click the Internet tab (**Figure 66**).

2. In Panther, choose either Built-In Ethernet or Internal Modem (whichever matches how you access the Internet) from the Share Your Connection From pop-up menu, and then select AirPort in the To Computers Using list.

3. If you want to enable DHCP service to provide IP addresses to client computers across both your wireless and your connected wired network, select Built-In Ethernet from the To Computers Using list. (Before enabling this option, read *Don't get your service canceled,* on page 38.)

Figure 66

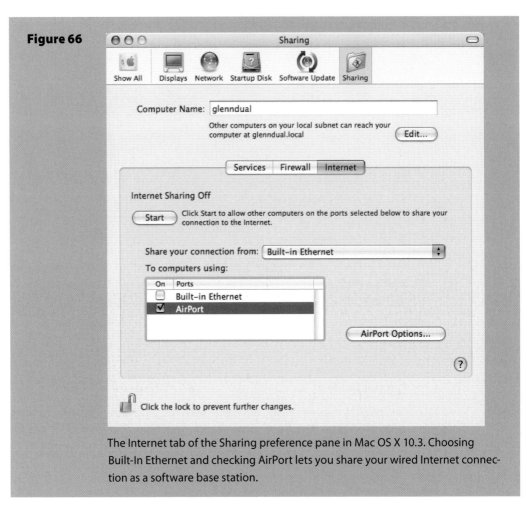

The Internet tab of the Sharing preference pane in Mac OS X 10.3. Choosing Built-In Ethernet and checking AirPort lets you share your wired Internet connection as a software base station.

4. Click AirPort Options to set the network name, channel, and WEP key (**Figure 67**).

5. Back in the Internet tab of the Sharing preference pane, click Start.

Figure 67

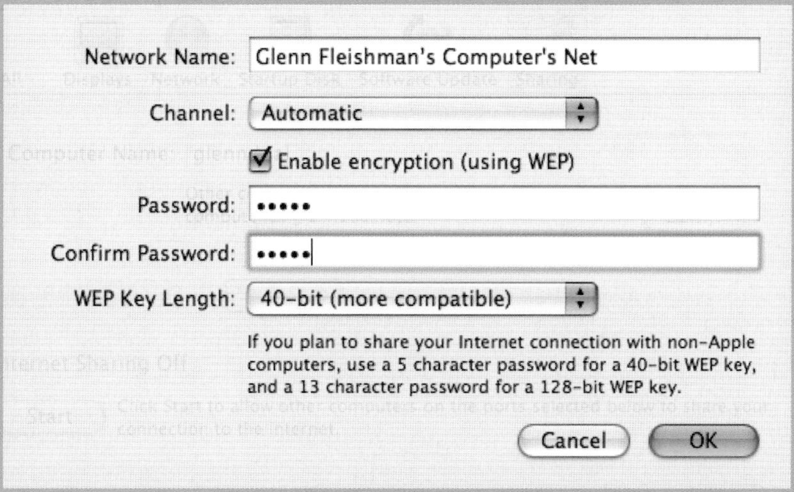

Network Name: Glenn Fleishman's Computer's Net

Channel: Automatic

☑ Enable encryption (using WEP)

Password: •••••

Confirm Password: •••••

WEP Key Length: 40–bit (more compatible)

If you plan to share your Internet connection with non-Apple computers, use a 5 character password for a 40–bit WEP key, and a 13 character password for a 128–bit WEP key.

Cancel   OK

Set the wireless options you want for your software base station, including a WEP password.

TIP   If you turn on WEP in Mac OS X 10.2 or 10.3 and anticipate PCs or Macs without AirPort cards ever wanting to access your network, I recommend you set the WEP key using a dollar sign, followed by the 10-digit or 26-digit hexadecimal key. When you type a dollar sign in a password field, the WEP Key Length menu dims and the OK button won't light up until you type the right number of identical digits in both password fields. I talk more about this issue in *Protect with WEP*.

Appendix C: Connect without AirPort Adapters

If you own a computer with an AirPort or AirPort Extreme slot but without a PC Card (CardBus) or PCI card slot, I recommend using an AirPort card from Apple. But if you have a slot free, you might consider a third-party alternative that could cost only $20 to $50.

OLDER POWER MACS THAT PREDATE AIRPORT

These computers can use Ethernet adapters, Wi-Fi PCI cards, and USB adapters, but each option comes with issues:

- A Wi-Fi Ethernet adapter like the 802.11b Linksys WET11 doesn't require specific Mac drivers like the cards do. You configure it with a Web interface. I recommend the WET11 for any older machine, including those that predate the PowerPC G3 processor and have 10Base-T Ethernet. A WET11 can bridge dozens of wired computers if you attach it to an Ethernet switch or hub, too (http://www.linksys.com/products/product.asp?grid=33&scid=36&prid=602).

  Don't bother with the 802.11g WET54G because these older Macs have only 10Base-T Ethernet, which runs at 10 Mbps, and is thus much slower than 802.11g's 54-Mbps throughput.

- If you are running Mac OS 8.6/9.x, you can use the 802.11b PCI card from MacWireless.com. It's a little expensive because it's unique (http://www.macwireless.com/html/products/11g_11b_cards/11bPCI.html).

- If you can run at least Mac OS X 10.2.8 and AirPort Software 3.1.1 or later on your older Power Mac, the 802.11g PCI cards made by Belkin, Buffalo, MacWireless.com, and Linksys work just as if they were AirPort Extreme Cards. No additional software is needed.

- If you lack a USB port, you could add a PCI card that provides USB (and FireWire, while you're at it) ports, and then use a Wi-Fi USB adapter from MacWireless.com or Belkin, as I describe next.

OLDER USB-ONLY IMACS

These computers lack the PCI slots of Power Macs, so you're down to either a Wi-Fi USB adapter or a Wi-Fi Ethernet adapter (such as the Linksys WET11, discussed just previously).

- Belkin (http://www.belkin.com/) now offers Mac OS X drivers for its Wi-Fi USB adapter, making it the best choice for putting an older iMac on a wireless network. Find the Belkin Mac OS 9.2 and X 10.1, 10.2, and 10.3 drivers at http://web.belkin.com/support/download/download.asp?download=F5D6050.

- MacWireless.com offers a USB adapter that has drivers for Mac OS 9.0.4 up to the latest releases of Mac OS X 10.3 (http://www.macwireless.com/html/products/11g_11b_cards/11bUSB.html).

- If you desperately want to make another vendor's USB adapter work with Mac OS X, and you're not afraid to get your hands virtually dirty, Thomas McQuitty has posted instructions on modifying the Belkin driver to work with a similar USB adapter from Netgear at http://www.mcquitty.net/Thomas/projects/USBWirelessOSX.html.

POWERBOOKS AND POWER MACS (G3 AND G4)

Any PowerBook or Power Mac that can run at least Mac OS 8.6 has one or more options that allow you to use the least expensive Wi-Fi adapter with your computer. In some cases, these adapters take advantage of Apple's built-in drivers, providing the best of both worlds.

Titanium PowerBooks are special candidates for these alternatives because of the heavy electromagnetic shielding the case provides and Apple's poor placement of the Wi-Fi antenna. (See *Solve the Titanium PowerBook Range Problem* for more information.)

- On PowerBooks running Mac OS X 10.2.8 and at least the AirPort Software 3.1.1 update, Apple's drivers automatically support 802.11g PC Cards from Belkin, Buffalo, Linksys, and MacWireless.com that use the Broadcom chip set.

- To use PC and PCI adapters from D-Link, NetGear, and others that use Atheros's chips with a proprietary faster Turbo mode (108-Mbps raw/30-odd-Mbps net), try OrangeWare's $15 driver. There's a free trial version. The driver supports the corporate 802.11a mode, and works with 802.11a/g dual-band cards, too (http://www.orangeware.com/endusers/wirelessformac.html).

- Mac OS 8.6/9.x and Mac OS X 10.1.5 or later users can also try the IOXperts $20 driver, which works with a large range of very cheap 802.11b cards. A trial version lets you test compatibility. See http://www.ioxperts.com/80211b.html for 8.6/9.x, and visit http://www.ioxperts.com/80211b_X.html for Mac OS X.

- If you use Mac OS 9 on a PowerBook, your best bet is to buy an Orinoco Silver or a WaveLAN Silver (same card, different name), since it uses the same hardware as Apple's AirPort cards and will work with Apple's AirPort drivers.

PCS RUNNING WINDOWS XP

Windows XP has terrific built-in support for Wi-Fi. Every piece of Wi-Fi equipment introduced in the last 2 years has a Windows XP driver; older equipment also often works without complaint. Because Wi-Fi is compatible across all manufacturers, you can use Windows XP computers to connect to AirPort networks.

PRE-WINDOWS XP PCS

An older Windows system can connect to AirPort only if you install a driver compatible with the particular system release, typically Windows 98 Second Edition (SE) through Windows 2000. Your best bet is probably the same recommendation I give for older PowerBooks: the Orinoco Silver or Gold adapter.

Appendix D: AirPort Management Tools

Apple released AirPort Management Tools 1.0 at the same time that they released AirPort Software 3.4. You can download the tools from `http://www.apple.com/support/airport/` by following a link in the Resources section at the right side of the Web page.

The tools comprise two packages:

- AirPort Client Monitor helps you monitor the ongoing signal and transmit rate; find out more in *Test with an AirPort or AirPort Extreme Card or compatible varieties.*

- AirPort Management Utility is a much more sophisticated package than the complex but one-base-station-at-a-time AirPort Admin Utility (which is part of the AirPort Software package). AirPort Management Utility eases the administration of many AirPort and AirPort Extreme Base Stations, as well as AirPort Express Base Stations in stand-alone mode or WDS mode.

USING AIRPORT MANAGEMENT UTILITY

AirPort Management Utility provides a number of distinct features:

- Discovering base stations on the local network via OpenTalk (née Rendezvous)

- Storing links to base stations by their IP addresses

- Allowing settings changes to apply to several base stations at once

- Storing configuration files for individual base stations, and storing model files that can be applied to new base stations

- Viewing logs of events at base stations, such as client associations and network time synchronization

- Monitoring signal strength over time of clients connected to a given base station, along with transfer statistics

The left bar of the AirPort Management Utility shows stored configuration files for base stations, base stations you've added manually by address that are stored in groups you define, and OpenTalk-enabled base stations that the program has discovered (**Figure 68**).

Figure 68

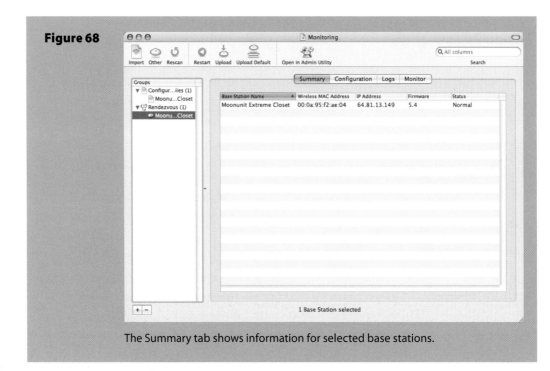

The Summary tab shows information for selected base stations.

ADDING A BASE STATION

There's no need to add base stations that AirPort Management Utility has discovered via OpenTalk (née Rendezvous), but if the utility doesn't see a base station with a static address, you can add it by clicking Other (in the toolbar) and then entering the IP address and password for the unit. When you click OK, the base station shows up in the list at left in a group called New Group. You can create your own groups and drag base stations in and out of them.

CONFIGURING ONE (OR MORE!) BASE STATIONS

Selecting one or more base stations and clicking the Configuration tab allows you to configure settings for one or more base stations at a time (**Figure 69**). For example, to change the DNS settings for all base stations on your network, you can simply enter them once and click Apply to cause all systems to reboot and have the new settings available.

Figure 69

The Configuration tab lets you change settings for one or more base stations at a time. Click the triangle next to each setting to choose specific base stations to which you want to apply a setting change.

You can also select a base station and click Open in Admin Utility (in the toolbar) to use the "traditional" configuration utility for a single base station at a time.

WORKING WITH A MODEL CONFIGURATION

You can export a configuration from AirPort Admin Utility and then import it into AirPort Management Utility to apply that model configuration to other base stations.

TIP　An irritating feature in AirPort Management Utility is that when you run it by itself, it opens with an Untitled window. You should save a document that contains all your settings for base stations and only open that document to use the AirPort Management Utility in the future. Otherwise you'll find yourself having to re-enter settings. (I recommend that you act on this tip before following the next set of steps.) You should also Save periodically while making changes to keep them tracked in the document.

To move a configuration from AirPort Admin Utility to AirPort Management Utility, follow these steps, starting from AirPort Management Utility:

1. Select the base station from the list at the left and click Open in Admin Utility (right side of toolbar) in order to connect to the base station.

2. Choose File > Save a Copy As. Name the file descriptively and save it in a place that's easy to find, such as the Desktop.

3. Switch back to AirPort Management Utility.

4. Click the Import button on the toolbar.

5. Navigate to and select the exported configuration file.

6. Click Open.

The file now appears in the list of Configuration Files.

LOGGING

The Logs tab shows information for a single base station, such as the association of wireless clients or reboot times (**Figure 70**). These logs can help you troubleshoot problems by providing specific information about what's happening in the base station.

Figure 70

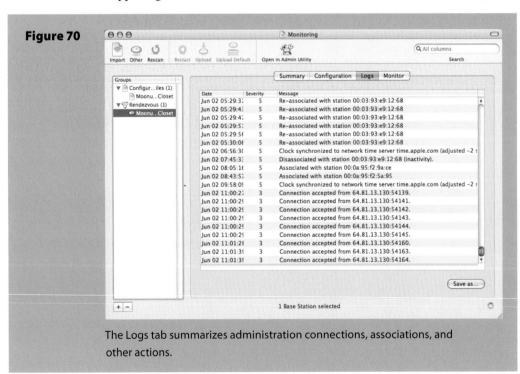

The Logs tab summarizes administration connections, associations, and other actions.

TIP The AirPort Extreme Base Station's 5.4 firmware lets you send the system messages shown in **Figure 70** to a syslog daemon, a common Unix server package that can receive messages and dump them to a text file. The syslog daemon typically gathers server reports of all kinds to provide a kind of central console.

MONITOR SIGNAL STRENGTH AND BYTES TRANSFERRED

Finally, you can use the Monitor tab to view the signal strength and bytes transferred for client connections to a given base station (**Figure 71**).

Figure 71

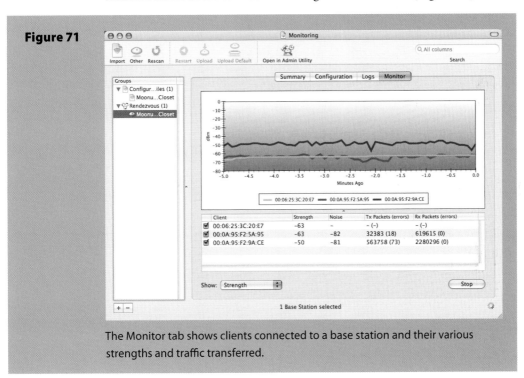

The Monitor tab shows clients connected to a base station and their various strengths and traffic transferred.

About the Author

Glenn Fleishman has written for hire since 1994, starting with *Aldus Magazine*. He contributes regularly to *Macworld*, *InfoWorld*, *PC World*, *The New York Times*, and *The Seattle Times*. He's the Macintosh columnist for *The Seattle Times*, and a contributing editor at *TidBITS* and *InfoWorld*.

Glenn spends much of his time writing about wireless networking. He co-wrote two editions of *The Wireless Networking Starter Kit* with Adam Engst (Peachpit Press, 2003 and 2004). He edits the daily Web log Wi-Fi Networking News (http://www.wifinetnews.com/), and he is the senior editor of Jiwire (http://www.jiwire.com/). He is also the author of *Take Control of Sharing Files in Panther*.

AUTHOR'S ACKNOWLEDGEMENTS

Thanks to Adam Engst, my editor and co-writer, for helping develop this title as a useful, self-contained book. Thanks also to my colleagues writing Take Control books; they are a wonderful, supportive group.

Index

H

hardware. *See also* **access points; adapters; Mac computers; wireless gateways**
adapters for Power Macs predating AirPort, 128
compatibility among AirPort devices, 7–8
firmware upgrades via Web browsers for non-Apple gear, 21
PowerBooks or Power Mac adapters, 129–130
pre-Windows XP PC adapters, 130
setting up shared USB printer, 60–62
USB-only iMac adapters, 128–129
using hard drives with USB port, 12
WDS options, 67, 69
wireless gateway support for AppleTalk, 22
hidden nodes, 67, 68
HomePlug bridges, 72–73

I

IEEE 802.1X with EAP
connecting Mac OS X 10.3 with, 92–96
defined, 91–92
difficulties enabling, 92
IEEE 802.11a standard, 8
IEEE 802.11b standard, 6, 7–8, 23, 64
IEEE 802.11g standard, 6, 7–8, 18, 64
IEEE 802.3af standard, 13
improving coverage area. *See also* **interference; WDS**
adding access points for roaming, 63–64
avoiding overlapping channels, 64
boosting signals with antenna, 73–74
Interference Robustness setting, 75–76
monitoring signal strength and bytes transferred, 135
neighborhood airspace testing, 76–77
PoE for exterior applications, 65
quick start tips, 4
solving range problems for Titanium PowerBook G4, 75
sources of Wi-Fi interference, 9
testing adapter signals, 27
WDS for, 65–72
Install AirPort 4.0 dialog, 101
installing
AirPort Express Base Station, 100–102
iTunes, 101
interference
sources of Wi-Fi network, 9
testing neighborhood airspace for, 76–77
Interference Robustness setting, 75–76
Internet connections, 29–59
about, 29
broadband modems to WAN port, 30–31
dealing with ISP MAC address access restrictions, 30, 33–34
DHCP configurations, 39–43
dial-up, 36–37
dynamically assigned addresses, 37–50
flowchart for, 30
log in via PPPoE over broadband DSL, 30, 32–33
passing traffic to computers on private networks, 50–59
receiving dynamic address over broadband, 30, 31–32
setting up, 111
software-based DHCP servers, 43–49
static addresses over broadband, 30, 34–36
Internet service providers. *See* **ISPs**
Internet Setup screen (AirPort Express Assistant), 111
Internet Sharing feature. *See also* **software base stations**
ISP problems with Internet Sharing and DHCP service, 37, 38–39
running DHCP and NAT server combination with Panther, 43, 44–45
setting up software base stations, 18, 19, 125–127
settings on Sharing preference pane, 45
Internet tab (AirPort Admin Utility), 116
Internet tab (Mac OS X 10.3), 126
IP addresses
allowing mixed static and dynamic, 35, 36
configuring static addresses, 48, 53–55
default Linksys WRT54G, 42, 43
distributing, 24, 107
dynamic address assignments with NAT and DHCP, 37–38
intermittent connectivity and changing, 20
non-routable private, 41
obtaining with bootp, 44
supplied by software base stations, 124
IPNetRouter, 125
IPNetRouterX
coupon for purchasing, 43, 46
using, 43, 46–48
iPod, 12
ISPs (Internet service providers)
Built-in Ethernet option and disruptions to, 44, 45
dealing with MAC address access restrictions, 30, 33–34
problems with Internet Sharing and DHCP service for, 37, 38–39
iTunes. *See also* **AirTunes**
installing, 101
setting up AirTunes, 14, 102, 119–122